Harry J Norton

Wonder-Land Illustrated

Or, HorsebackRides through theYellowstone National Park

Harry J Norton

Wonder-Land Illustrated

Or, HorsebackRides through theYellowstone National Park

ISBN/EAN: 9783337211394

Printed in Europe, USA, Canada, Australia, Japan

Cover: Foto ©Andreas Hilbeck / pixelio.de

More available books at **www.hansebooks.com**

WONDER-LAND

ILLUSTRATED;

OR,

HORSEBACK RIDES

THROUGH THE

YELLOWSTONE NATIONAL PARK.

BY HARRY J. NORTON.

HARRY J. NORTON:
VIRGINIA CITY, MONTAÑA.

PREFACE.

This little volume is published for the satisfaction of the author, and at the request of many of his personal friends. He claims no especial literary merit for it, but simply that it contains a very complete unscientific, but truthful account and description of the many wonders of the Yellowstone National Park. It will also be found valuable as a guide-book for tourists, as it gives a minute description of the trail over the Grand Rounds, distances from point to point, cost of making the trip, etc. The Yellowstone National Park is a tract of land situate on the sources of the Yellowstone and Madison rivers, and is fifty-five by sixty-five miles in extent. It was set aside from pre-emption and settlement by an act of the second session of the Forty-second Congress, and is just now being brought into prominent notice. In acknowledgment for personal favors, he is pleased to mention Dr. F. V. HAYDEN, U. S. Geologist, from whose annual reports he has gleaned much valuable information and data; Mr. JAMES STEVENSON, Dr. Hayden's assistant; Gen. B. R. COWEN, Acting Secretary of the Interior; the ILLUSTRATED CHRISTIAN WEEKLY and Messrs. SCRIBNER & ARMSTRONG, New York, for illustrations; and his brethren of the press in Montana. His Letters were first written for the Virginia City MONTANIAN, and are published without a revision. With this brief explanation he takes pleasure in introducing the reader to his companions on the "Horseback Rides through the National Park."

H. J. NORTON, AUTHOR.

VIRGINIA CITY, MONTANA, 1873.

THE WONDERS

OF

WONDER-LAND.

A Trip to The Geysers. — Horseback Rides through the National Park.

LETTER NO. I.

THE first paragraph of this letter is intended to be purely apologetic. It is with an acute consciousness of the utter weakness of our own intellect, and a regretful enviousness of the descriptive powers of our literary superiors, that we attempt the narration of our eventful journey to, and a portrayal of the many wondrous beauties seen on our recent trip through the Wonder-land of the universe. Do we attempt to concentrate our ideas and mould them into comprehensive sentences, they instantly dissolve into the vapor of imagination, and we gaze only upon the chaotic confusion of a mind conscious of its own complete bewilderment. In such a dilemma, if we would make ourselves understood, we can but passively follow the briefly-recorded notes of our journeying, dodging out occasionally from the beaten trail for elaboration, and appealing to the imagination of our readers as we get lost amid the entangling brushwood of details. So much in apology, and we proceed as best we may.

The Geyser Exploring Party, organized and equipped at Virginia, Montana, on the 3d and 4th of the present month, (September, 1872,) was entirely *impromptu*, and consisted of the following persons: Capt. Jas. H. Mills, editor of the (Deer Lodge) *New Northwest;* P. A. Largey, Esq., of the Deer Lodge and Bozeman Telegraph Lines, (who will sometimes be mentioned in these letters as "Prince Telegraph;) Dr. M. H. Raymond of Kentucky; Messrs. Hillhouse Raymond, Frank Woodall, Theo. Freeler, and the writer, of Virginia. Hurried and incomplete preparations were made on the evening of the third and morning after, and at two o'clock on the afternoon of Wednesday the party were in the saddle urging three pack-animals, laden with commissary stores and bedding, towards the summit of the Madison divide. It was with no small degree of charity that we heartily forgave the waggishness of our equininical friend, Tom Farrell, in constructing and mounting on a degenerate-looking crow-bait that man of straw, labelled the "Geyser-Guide," and with the same overflow of sacrificed pride said Amen to the hilarity of our witnessing lady acquaintances who viewed the ludicrous and novel situation of affairs from a neighboring store-window. Our hearts were bent on beholding the wonders of Geyser-land, and the suppressed "te-hees" and "ha-has" of the assembled spectators only added to our impatience to be well out of sight.

An easy drive took us over the Madison divide and to a camp at English George's, on the Madison river, at 6 P. M. The first night out promised to be a rather rough one on our little band of shorn lambs. Indeed, it is presumed that "the first night out" for the entire human race is proverbially unhappy, and that our experience in this regard is not very far beyond the average. The animals unpacked, supper despatched, and the blankets spread on the grass, we sought our first night's slumber beneath a deeply-clouded sky, a few lonely little stars the while twinkling their rays of hope, and persuading us that the ominous rain-clouds would not burst until morning. It was not long, however, ere the few peeping stars ceased to shine, the clouds opened, and the rain came down in torrents, compelling us to seek shelter beneath the hospitable roof of our hunter friend, where we passed the remainder of the night quite cosily.

Breakfast over, the morning found us wending our way up the west bank of the Madison river at the rate of four miles per hour. This was on the 5th, and there is little worthy of record save Ruby creek and cañon, fifteen miles above our camp of the 4th. This creek flows into the Madison from the west, and in seeking the society of its nobler sister, carves a gateway through a precipitate bluff of over two hundred feet in height, forming one of the most weird and romantic cañons ever beheld. There seems a sacred silence encircling this beauteous bower, as if the amorous gods had there built a trysting-place to woo and win their fairy loves, and from every velvety, verdure-clad nook, in its impenetrable windings, there seems to be wafted the soft pleadings of the whispering lovers. This mysteriously beautiful cluster of Nature's architectural handiwork is deserving of admiration, and no doubt attracts every one who passes that way as it did us.

The trail thence to Wire creek, our next camp, leads over valley, along hillside, and through cañon, alternately, for five miles. It is a delightful portion of the country, and has its share of natural ornamentation. A short distance from the creek the trail winds through a sequestered vale, dotted here and there with huge boulders of honeycomb-rock.

Prominent among these gigantic relics of the olden days, when classical giants played from "taw" with small mountains, and took their "slings" with rocks in 'em, is a monster granite formation, in shape very like an "A" tent, which of course challenged the A-tent-ion of the battle-scarred heroes of the cavalcade as it passed.

Just beyond Wire creek, on a low hill, we notice the first indication of geyser formation in a small group of almost extinct mud-springs, in which can yet be discerned the last feeble pulsations of active eruption. Years must have elapsed since these mud volcanoes were in violent action, as the exterior of the mounds and the lava on the plateau below have become dry and flinty, and the shrubbery surrounding them thrifty and rank-grown.

In approaching our camp at the mouth of Madison cañon, and while feeling our way down a sharp declivity of rocks, the horse of Capt. Mills made a false step, violently dumping his attenuated burden upon the sharp and uncushioned terra firma. Fortunately no bones were broken, but that bruised and bleeding shank—a figurative spring radish with a strip of peeling taken off—was the means by which we learned how complete is the triumph of mind over matter. On riding ahead and informing the junior of our party—a young man who goes his "A.sic" on emetics and cosmetics—that our favorite Bohemian had met with a severe accident, with a confident and Esculapian wave of the hand he exclaimed, "Ah, how fortunate that I brought my Magic Ointment!" and without inquiring whether the injury sustained was a bunged eye or a broken collar-bone, he thrust the specific upon us.

The next camp was made after crossing the river to the east side, the watery transit being accomplished with no other loss than that of our camp-kettle, the finding of which an hour afterward put good spirits into the party again, and afforded our telegraphic friend an opportunity of claiming a double ration of something held in solution by an iron-corseted gallon keg.

The forenoon of the following day was occupied in passing the second Madison cañon. We do not recollect of having heard or read anything descriptive of this magnificent passage-way through the mountains, but really cannot conceive how an appreciative traveller could follow on through its miniature forests, its grass-grown glades, over its narrow, rock-paved trail that now and then clings to the steep mountain sides midway between heaven and earth, without being vividly impressed with its indescribable beauty and grandeur. The cañon proper is about eight miles in length, and varies from a few yards to half a mile in width. The coloring throughout is agreeable to the eye; and in places where it narrows to its closest contraction, the sombre shadows cast over its diminutive belt of mingled purple, green, and golden vestures by the towering and precipitous walls of black rock on either side, lends an additional enchantment to the picture. The narrow, rock-ribbed pass is supplied with many clear, ice-cold springs, whose crystal waters seem ever inviting thirst for the beneficent object of slaking it from the wealth of their delectable fountains. At a point midway of the cañon on the east side, at no less altitude than one thousand feet above the river bed, there juts out from the black wall a stream of spring-water some six or eight feet in width, and dashing down the almost perpendicular plane, finds its way to the vale below in mist, vapor, and foam, there to again form into water and plunge into a sink leading underground to the river. The stream, as it leaps down the mountain, adds a new splendor to the picturesque scene, resembling a stream of molten silver being ejected from its eyrie crucible.

One would naturally suppose elk, deer, and

mountain-sheep would seek a home in this sheltered nook of the forest; but if such is their habit, it was their visiting-season, as we saw no living thing during our ride through save two sour-looking timber-wolves, who scampered affrightedly away at our approach.

Passing out of the cañon, the trail leads along the river into a fine bottom, called by old trappers the Fire-Hole Basin. Whether it has gained this appellation from its close proximity to the Geysers or from the scorched appearance of the soil and a greater portion of its surroundings, we are not informed, but the evidences of its having been at one time subjected to intense heat are abundant throughout.

Farther on up the basin we cross the east fork of the river, ascend a timbered divide separating the east and west branches, and finally descend the bank of the west branch, which now takes the name of Fire-Hole river. As the stream is approached we behold a succession of gentle cascades, over which the bright waters go gleefully dancing and singing like some merry maiden who, care-free, trips her way to receive the garland of flowers which shall crown her Queen of the May.

The trail over this heavily-timbered dividing ridge is the only portion of the route which we remember as having been "blazed" by the explorer's axe. At intervals of fifty or a hundred feet along the narrow zigzag bridle-path the trees have been blazed (hacked) by Mr. Langford's little hatchet for future guidance. How vividly this incident recalled to mind our youthful endeavors to "blaze" such a moral trail through the intricate wilderness of sin and temptation through which we were called to pass in the halcyon days of our boyhood, as should cause our associates to see and avoid it as the "trail of the serpent!" But alas for human exertion to bequeath to posterity a blessing! They would not. We had

HALFWAY SPRINGS, FIRE-HOLE RIVER.

incubated our brilliant and charitable idea prematurely, for most of our benighted fellow-mortals naturally take the beaten trail, rather than strike out in the wilderness on their own hook. Well, while we have made a failure through life in this great aim, we have the consolation of knowing that "a heap" of jolly, good fellows are plodding along over our old trail, and like us, patiently waiting an opportunity to throw the "diamond hitch" over their share of godliness and greenbacks.

Fire-Hole river, five miles farther down called the Madison, is not here noticeably reduced in size, although it has divided its waters with its largest tributary, but still retains a noble volume of water. Just above the cascades, and directly opposite a small, almond-shaped island, we relieved the pack-horses of their burdens and camped for the night. Great was the speculation around the camp-fire that evening, for on the morrow the goal so anxiously sought would be ours. Two of the party, more roamantically inclined, had crossed over to the little island and built their camp-fire beneath the shadows of its many trees. They returned to us in the morning with glowing descriptions of the sighing and singing of the merry water-sprites who lulled them to sleep in their island couch, and had we not known the doctor to be manacled by conjugal restrictions, we would think it possible that a veritable Undine had wooed him to slumber in her loving arms.

On the morning of the 9th we were again in the saddle, pushing on for the Geysers, and it was during our trip to the lower basin over an exceedingly muddy trail that the genial Prince Telegram solved to our satisfaction the question of "cruelty to animals." On the third day out his cayuse had become entangled in a lariat, and before it could be rescued had pawed its head to a jelly. In fact, it was a "first-class head." Riding up behind the Prince, we overheard the following apostrophe: "O horse! O ca-

1*

yuse! how nimbly didst thou caper ere the carelessness of thy master didst inflict those terrible wounds! Thy head, ay, even thy tail was erect, and did battle gloriously with the cruel bluebottle, whose sting is more powerful for evil than the kick of a jassack! Now, alack, thy head draggeth the ground like an odometer, and has increased in size many fold! Thy tail is limp, and thy ear heeds no legend but that of *w'oa!* Verily thou art 'petered,' and my soul weepeth for pity; but it is muddy, my boots are full of vents, and I'll just be *dogoned* if I get off and walk! There are thousands of you, and but one of me—yea, I will keep my sitting!" That last argument was a clincher, and gave the listener absolution for riding a sore-backed horse through the same slough.

The party arrived at lower Geyser Basin for dinner, meeting *en route* a party of gentlemen from Helena under the benign guidance of Bishop Bullock. Their enthusiastic accounts of the wonders seen but gave our anxiety a keener impatience, and the halt was too brief to exchange the roll-calls.

LETTER NO. II.
PRESTO! A CHANGE OF SCEPTRES.

Look cautiously, tread carefully—for we are now in the enchanted land, surrounded on every side with mystery and marvel. One brief hour has sufficed to change our quiet, love-inspiring, soul-entrancing scenery into that of a land of awe and wonder. The natural king has faded from our vision, and the supernatural monarch has ascended the throne with glittering crown, and with magic wand is ever directing our footsteps through his mystic domain. One hour since we were tracing the emerald-shaded, grass-carpeted bank of a placid, smiling river—listening to its soft, soothing carols as it quietly gurgled its good-bys to the bold mountain-peaks under whose shadows it passed; now singing merrily, now echoing its everlasting Nevermore to the dainty little rivulets as each one, tired of wandering, glided from its gloomy cañon and buried itself in her broad, matronly bosom. One hour! and the Queen of Quiet has lain down her sceptre of loving order, and the King of Confusion and Passion reigns supreme.

But hold; we forget that you, our reader, may perhaps be a novice, and have never yet stepped within the dominions of this modern Pluto, and that we who have taken the degrees of his mystical lodge are talking in riddles. Let us for a moment forget our wonderment as the mysteries of his realm were unfolded to us, and endeavor to explain what we saw.

Letter No. One left us just making an entry into the lower Geyser Basin. On emerging from the timber which everywhere thickly studs the river bank from the island and cascades to the mouth of the cañon, we were greeted by a column of steam ascending in front and just a little to the right of us. On approaching, we caught our first glimpse of hot water in a moderate-sized boiling spring, located some rods from the river bank, and around which a considerable mound had formed. It may as well be said now as at any other time, that these hot-spring mounds all partake of the same nature in material, and are indisputably formed by the constant overflow and deposit of sediment contained in the water. The predominating minerals or materials contained in the water and in the deposits of these hot-springs and geysers, are said to be lime, soda, alumina, magnesia, sulphur, and silica; but we make no pretensions to being a scientist, and for aught we know to the contrary, they may be a solution of sardonic smiles, and flimsy fabrics of fairy phantoms held in a liquid state by a confluence of their own and some other fellow's affidavit. That's all we know about calcareous deposits and other things, and we propose to elaborate our ideas independent of science, taking the chances that some of our readers will appreciate it above an ostentatious display of "big words."

The mound of this spring had grown into a little eminence of ten feet in height, and perhaps fifty feet in circumference at the base. The spring itself did not strike us as being particularly wonderful, and, as we afterward ascertained by comparison, was one of the most inferior in the basin. A few hundred yards farther on we found a handsomely-formed white sulphur spring imbedded in the river-bank, the nearest portion of its curiously-scalloped rim reaching to within six inches of the water of the river. This formation much resembled a huge oblong shell, and was completely lined inside with a creamy-white coating formed by the adhesion of the sulphurous sediment to its wall. The waters were hot, perfectly transparent, and gave forth a strong odor of sulphur. Of course it was a subject of much delight and enthusiasm; but our party soon wearied of its attractions, and struck out in search of bigger wonders. We could now see columns of steam ascending in many directions, and as we followed the well-beaten trail, came upon a great number of small and large hot-springs, varying more or less in form and character from the one already described. The waters of some were insipid, others tasteless, while others were even nauseous, from the abundance of mineral solution contained. Among the objects of interest found on our first entering the basin, was a small mud-geyser, or mud-puff, situated at the base of a high bank, which, when we arrived, was sputtering away like a small-fry politician. In distinction to the hot-springs, these mud-pots are invariably located in a depression or sink, and no mound of any height is formed. Its ebullition was constant, and the ground round about gave forth a hollow, rumbling sound. In endeavoring to gain a close view of it, Dr. Raymond rode his horse into the outer edge of the vat, and in an instant found himself sinking into the soft, mushy substance. The hot mud acted like percussion to the animal, as he sprang out with a bound, and with hind-legs completely coated with the clayey paste. From this point to the upper end of the basin, where the most prominent springs are situated, there is a succession of hot water urns on both banks of the river—some bubbling gently, and others boiling violently and overflowing to the river. These urns, or basins, are of a variety of color, and of many shapes; the tendency, however, is to a circular form. The basin of one is shaped much like a funnel, is about six feet in diameter, with waters clear as crystal thirty or forty feet in depth, and the sides are lined with a delicate white enamel resembling porcelain. The temperature of these springs is said by Prof. Hayden to vary from 112° to 197°. Pine boughs or other material, when held under the hot water for any length of time, become completely coated with an incrustation of white silica, and wood petrifactions are abundant throughout the whole region. Among other curious formations in this portion of the basin is what is known as the "Catfish Geyser," though the resemblance to its piscatorial namesake is not remarkable. It is located in the very water's edge of the river, has thrown up a curiously-shaped dome of nearly eight feet in height, and boils continuously. The crater is not over six feet in circumference, but its inside lining is unique and pretty. We do not know that it has stated intervals of spouting, or even that it spouts at all. Its ebullitions are at times sufficiently violent to throw the water three or four feet above the crater, and the amount of sediment about the mound indicates that if it does not now, it has done considerable spouting in its palmy days. In this respect it is not vastly different from some politicians we wot of, who have literally spouted themselves to exhaustion in the effort to shoot a great ball a long distance out of a small calibre. Each wonder was inspected and admired in turn, as we slowly passed to the upper end of the basin, where apparently the elements were in greatest commotion. Picking out a suitable place blessed with shade and luxuriant grass, we camped for dinner, determining to explore the large upper section to the left in the afternoon. These out-door repasts were always despatched with an avidity that would lead a spectator to the belief that each member of our little expedition, like our unfortunate friend T. C. Evarts, the "champion lost man of the National Park," had just emerged from his "thirty-seventh day of peril."

It is a gentle ascent all the way from our camp to the upper section referred to, and the ground is either boggy or completely covered with a parti-colored crust of sedimentary deposits from the overflowing geysers and springs. Through the cap or crust there are numerous vents through which the steam escapes with a hissing, vicious noise, as if a thousand little valves were continually being tried by the chief engineer of the concern to ascertain how much pressure his infernal machine was running on.

Situated at the summit of the eminence is a boiling lake of nearly four hundred feet in circumference, with a beautifully-tinted and ruffled rim, and with waters so clear that, standing on its margin, one can look into its crystal depths for many fathoms. Its curious basin is adorned with more brilliant colors and decorations than any structure which the human mind can imagine. Near by is the Fountain Geyser, Architectural Fountain, Thud Geyser, and many other noticeable springs. Anything like an accurate description of these numerous curiosities would occupy a much larger space than we care to take, and they must therefore be left to the imagination of the reader. There is only one more marvel which we cannot pass without an attempt to describe before leaving the Lower Basin. This is an immense boiling chalk-vat, a short distance south of Fountain Geyser. It is perhaps the most remarkable feature in the basin. It is oblong in form, has a diameter within the rim or wall forty by sixty feet, and is apparently very deep. The rim is three to five feet in height, and nearly perpendicular to the surface of the solution.

The ebullition is not very violent, but more like huge bubbles rising slowly to the surface and exploding with a puffing sound. The escapes are so numerous and the puffing so continuous, that the vat has the appearance of boiling. At each bubble-burst a spirt of hot chalk is thrown two or three feet above the surface, and falling back, keeps up a constant sputter and spatter. To Prof. Hayden it is " an impalpable, silicious clay," but to an unlearned mind it is *chalk*, with colors of every shade, from a bright, rich pink to a snowy-white—each color distinct from and independent of the others. The wall is of the same material, and sufficiently hardened to admit of being cut into square blocks with a pocket-knife.

After lunching our curiosity, (for there is no such thing as *satiating* it in the midst of so many wonders,) we saddled up and started for the upper Geyser Basin. The distance between the two basins is called nine miles, and the trail keeps along a muddy, heavily-timbered bottom close to the river for most of the way. We would not think the two basins entirely independent of each other, notwithstanding so great a distance intervenes, but are of the opinion that numerous subterranean channels act as feeding arteries of steam and water between the two, creating a common sympathy and a common diabolism. Indeed, there is good reason for this theory, if not for the one that the whole underground-area of the Geyser region is an immense boiling lake (of "fire and brimstone"), without other vent or outlet than the fissures apparent on the ground surface.

At one or two points on the journey to the upper basin we found boiling-springs similar to those we had before seen. In one place the river-bank for several hundred feet was gorgeous with the many-colored incrustations and the large volume of hot water flowing from one of the gigantic springs located on the west bank.

It was nearly night of September 10 when we reached the upper basin, and fording the river to its west shore, found a suitable camping-place in a small grove of tall, rugged pines, some fifty yards distant from what has been named by the Langford party as the Castle Geyser. On first entering, the entire basin seemed enveloped in steam, and from a thousand vents the heated vapor ascended through the gray evening twilight to the blue and cloudless sky above. The scene was grand, imposing, and im-

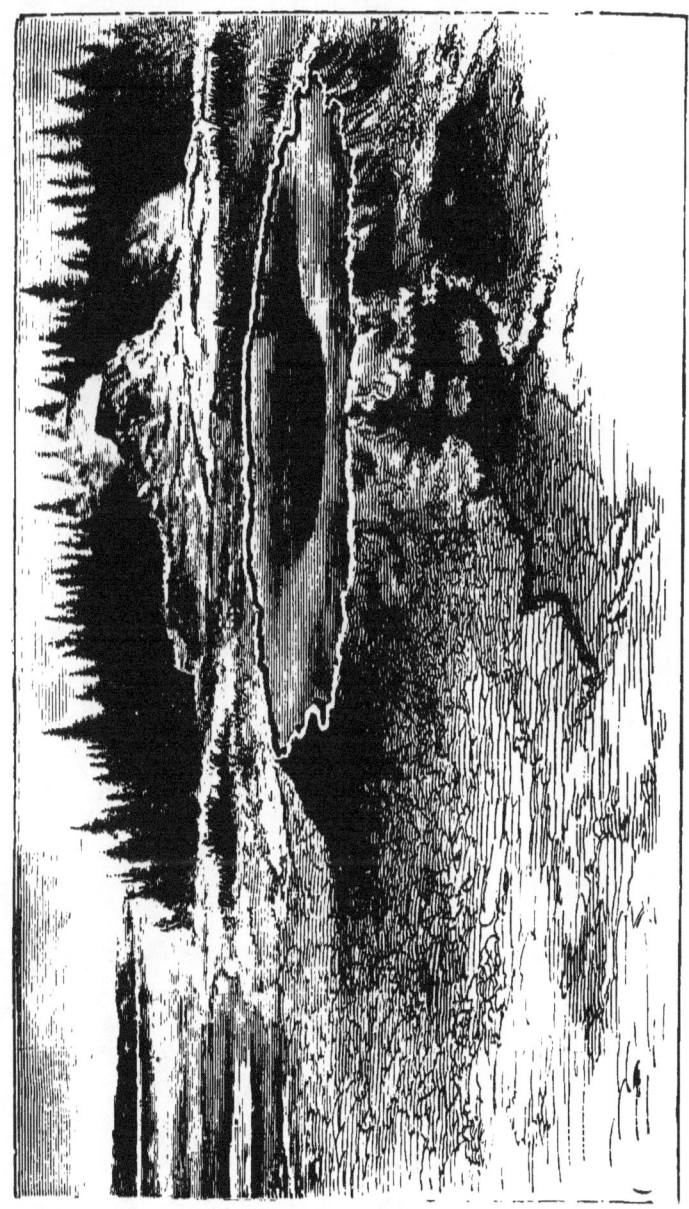

CASTLE GEYSER.

pressive. That which we had wondered at in the basin below was here magnified a thousand-fold, and in comparison dwindled into insignificance and forgetfulness. That was beautiful and wonderful; this was grand, majestic, sublime. As soon as the animals were unpacked, and before preparations were made for supper, the whole party impatiently rushed off to have a look at the old monster, Castle Geyser. This formation much resembles the ruins of some ancient castle, and looms up fully twenty feet above its mound in a cunningly-carved and oddly-fashioned chimney, with its terraces and steps in regular succession leading downward. The silicious deposits have taken a great variety of shapes, and all around the dome crystals have formed in beauteous profusion. The crater or orifice through which the boiling water is forced is about two and a half by five feet in diameter, and gorgeously ornamented reservoirs of whitest and daintiest lining receive the waters as they fall with continual plashings from the turbulent fountain. A grumbling, angry sound is constantly heard within the chimney, and its muttered threatenings often terminate in a deafening roar and violent expulsion of steam and water. At the only times we witnessed its eruption the column ascended not over sixty feet, and continued seven minutes, but maybe it was not then doing its "level best."

CIRCE'S BOUDOIR.

"Thereby hangs a tale."

Upon the same mound, a few steps from the Castle, is one of those calm, lovely prismatic springs, the most beautiful in the whole geyser region. For delicacy of coloring and beauty of ornamentation it surpasses any we visited. It is more quiet than the others, yet its surface is gently rippled by constant vibrations. The handsomely-scalloped rim rises seven or eight inches above the water, describes a complete circle of about sixty feet, and inside is festooned and embroidered in many a fantastic design. The water is unnaturally transparent, and one can look an unknown depth into its fairy regions, discovering caves, bowers, castles, and grottoes, painted in every color of brightest rainbow, and magically carved, as though it had, as indeed it has, received the most exquisite touches of the Great Master Artist. Standing on its margin, and gazing enraptured into its unfathomable depths, one becomes enchanted with this delightful realm, and calls to mind all that he has ever heard or read about the airy phantoms and ogling water-sprites of mythological tales. It seemed as if our eyes would never cease feasting upon its unearthly beauty; there was an intense longing to know what mysterious treasures lie hidden deep down in its tranquil bosom; and as we regretfully, unsatisfiedly retired to rest, we wondered who would care if we explored its deepest recesses—to return to earth never again! Weary with the day's explorations, we were soon wrapped in profound slumber, keeping time and tune with the nasal notes of our already snoring companions. How long we slept we know not, but our mind would not rest, and we awoke with brain busily at work on mysteries and theories, and with increased longing to again visit the bewitching spectacle which had so impressed us before retiring. So irresistible was this desire, that we determined to arise and again gaze into its dreamy waters.

"Now Night had shed her silver dews around,
And with her sable wings embraced the ground;
Underneath a cloud the moon had gone,
But brighter shone the stars so left alone."

Pale-faced Diana, in her trackless flight through the ethereal monuments of heaven, cast a trembling, green-gray shadow on the deep shade of night, causing the strange and wonderful surroundings to appear, if possible, more weird and supernatural. Old Faithful's* deep-toned cough echoed and re-echoed from bluff to bluff, and the regular pulsations of the Fan Geyser seemed to skip from cliff to cliff, like the Peri seeking the gift most dear to heaven. Unearthly objects flitted past, merging into one another, dimly descried—confusedly lost sight of—gone! Occasionally a sigh of mountain-air came from the distant snow-capped peaks, and shifting images rose up in my fancy, and vanishing, left a chill upon my blood. Long I stood debating what to do, but at length determined to accomplish my purpose. Tremblingly I took my way toward the miniature lakelet, when the strangest of all strange sights I saw. Clustered around the water's edge were a bevy of water-nymphs, and in the centre Circe herself! with halo-light flashing from her brow, her white limbs, like Parian marble, showing through her thin attire that seemed a golden mist. And while I stood amazed, straining my ear to hark, scarce sure, I heard veiled, sweet voices around the silvery fount, that shed strange, fitful music, more beautiful than tongue can tell, while the confused twitter of the restless birds

"Within their temples, groves of ancient trees,
Accompanied the soft, silvery evening breeze.
'T was surely the siren's song I heard,
Though ear could shape it to no word."

On seeing me, a mortal, they became frightened, and softly from the unique bank they slid, and with small noise disappeared in the gurgling water, save one, whose gray eyes and yellow hair made her more beautiful than all the rest, who stole silently from out the pool, and in a moment was at my side! Around her dimpled limbs, worthy of the sea-born queen, hung a frock of gauzy gold, strange of its fashion,

* The most important geyser in the basin, throwing an immense volume of hot water to the height of 175 feet once every 67 minutes. This and other geysers will be noticed in Letter III.

and about her blazed many a fair gem and outlandish stone. Her hands seemed very ivory, and her cheek as fair as any god has kissed—eyes that were languid, liquid stars, and lovely neck half covered with a wealth of golden hair.

"Mortal," said she, "your intrusion at this hour and on this sacred spot deserves severer punishment than that even dealt by the virgin goddess to the prying Actæon for intruding on her privacy, but the fates on this occasion seem to be in your favor, for on this our queen's natal day ill or woe cannot bide in her domain. And since you are here under these circumstances, and as we immortals know you have an unusual and inordinate desire to explore the depths of yon crystal fount, I have my lady's word that you not only can but shall see all the mysteries it gives entrance to. But ere I take you from this mundane sphere, let me say that you are now on hallowed ground. Immediately beneath us are the abodes of the gods, Mount Olympus and the Elysian Plains; and yonder virgin water you mortals call a spring is the terrestrial entrance to the celestial world. Old Pluto's belch you call a geyser, and the overplus sulphurous matter ejected from Hecate's caldron through yonder orifice you misname a mineral spring; and your mud-volcanoes are but the vain Chimera's vomitings.

"When, oh when will your mortal world become more wise? Even your demigod, *Gov. Langford*, 's a fool in *our* eyes!

"But come, without further delay I will lead you first to the blessed realm, and then to Erebus we will go; and fortunate are you, for no mortal since Æneas has been so favored by the gods."

Shivering and shaking in every limb, overspread with a damp sweat and holy fear, I would have retreated, but the fates were at work, and I strove in vain. Daintily my lovely guide reached her slim palm to mine, and with its touch I felt as through

my blood strange fire ran. She led the way, and I,
now a willing follower, was by her side. Around
her slender waist I put my arm, and fearlessly into
the unfathomable transparency we leaped, going
down, down, down, locked in each other's arms!

At length to a huge adamantine gate we came,
With golden pillars capped with rubies rare ;
My fair enchantress-guide but waved her hand, and open
    wide it flew,
But not a drop of water passed there through!

"Had I a hundred mouths, a hundred tongues,
A throat of brass inspired with iron lungs,"
I could not half of beauties there repeat,
Nor half the grandeur that my eyes there met.
Crystal streams that murmured through the meads,
Ether-vested and purple skies,
Verdant fields filled with myriads of happy things,
And gods and goddesses.

In no fixed place the happy souls reside ;
In groves they all abide.
And lie on mossy beds softer than eider down.

There, dreaming on a bed of daisies cold,
"Hedged round about with woodbine and red rose,
Near to a marble fountain's plashing rim,
Whose broken waves goldfish showed dim,
Within the flicker of a white-thorn shade,"
In gentle sleep I found fair Venus laid.

And just before the confines of a wood,
Where gliding Lethe leads her gentle flood,
Eros, the god of love, stood, not alone,
For now he calls immortalled Psyche all his own.

Deep in a shaded myrtle-grove
Virgin Diana toys with a dove ;
And Juno, queen, with Iris by her side,
Her fair face flushed with sweet thoughts, like a bride
Lovely she looked, the while the moonlight ran
In silvery riplets o'er her lily hand.

Far in a cool and silent wood
The golden temple of Apollo stood ;
Within the wooded deep did strange birds sing,
Praising the god in their sweet carolling.

We entered softly, and with trembling hand
And holding breath, "the wonder of all land
Met here the wonder of the lands and sea."

Fragrant and dainty flowers from Cyprus brought,
And curious stones most wonderfully wrought;
Tapestried chambers with figures of bright gold,
And silvery hangings, did our eyes behold.

"In a separate grove, through which a gentle breeze
Plays with a passing breath that whispers through the trees,"
The nymphs and fairies in grottoes there reside,
But from a mortal's eyes they always hide.

Great Jove, in all his splendid guise,
We wished to see and satiate our eyes;
But Circe told us that could never be,
And brought to mind the fate of Semele.

At length we came to where the dreadful Styx doth glide,
And found in different paths the way divide;
The one to that unhappy region runs
Where Pluto's horrid reign has but begun.

As we drew near the Stygian flood, the demoniac yells of the damned were plainly heard. Grim, triple-mouthed Cerebus, with snaky neck, belched from each head a deathlike, savage howl. I was here charged by my fair guide to summon up all my courage; "for," said she, "you will now require it." The air was black as midnight, yet all things were discernible through it. The flaming Phlegathron lighted up its own turbid waves, but the glare extended no farther. Old Charon, with hoary chin and unkempt hair, alone mans his leaky craft at Cocytus. Busy is he with travellers going over, but never one is there that comes back. Revenge, Care, Sorrow, Famine, Disease, the horrid Hydra, Gorgons, and Death, just in the jaws of Hell, with ravenous desires, stand ready to possess all who enter into their domain.

As we proceeded farther, respiration became almost impossible, and the air was thick with sulphurous soots. The groans of the ghosts and wails of souls lost for ever, seen and heard, were more horrible than even Danté pictures. Salmonius we saw racked with agonizing pain, Ixion on the ever-moving wheel, and Prometheus with the vulture gnawing his liver—devoured, but never growing less; and Tantalus, with parched lips and bloodshot eyes, longing for water always in sight but never in reach!

On a throne of burnished gold inlaid with diamonds of black and yellow hue sat Pluto and his stolen bride and consort, Proserpine. On every side are huge caldrons of molten iron, in which are writhing millions of human souls!

My fair conductress here paused and said:

"This repulsive region is the source and cause of the so-called mysteries in your admired Geyser-land, and the steam and heat and groans of the Giantess, Giant, and Castle geysers are produced by the burning of souls and bodies such as yours; and you mortals, while gazing at the mysteries of that country, are indirectly witnessing the everlasting punishment of friends and relatives.

"But come," said she, "your eyes are growing strange, and a farther sight of this damnable place would be too much for your mortal body." With this she hurried me away.

Half dead with fatigue and fright, my strength failed on the way, and I should certainly have perished had not, through Circe's wiles, Mercury, the messenger of the gods, been induced to take me on his shoulders and bear me to the outer world. I gladly climbed up on his back, one hand meanwhile tenaciously grasping the gift of Proserpine, a golden lyre.

Just then I felt an unmerciful poke in the ribs, opened wide my eyes, and discovered myself astride of Pat Largey's shoulders, and my right hand clutched into the brown locks of my friend, Capt. Mills. *I had been dreaming!*

LETTER NO. III.

The impressions made upon my mind by the underground tour with that bewitching, golden-haired sprite—Circe, the enchantress guide of my slumbering vision—has since been dispelled; but the realities beheld in that beautiful spring will not soon be forgotten. There are many other remarkable springs in the upper basin, but as each one in description must needs be a reflection of another, their further portrayal will be dispensed with.

Just for the oddity of the idea, some of the party proposed next day at dinner that we should try a cup of geyser tea. Happy thought! a million billion barrels of hot water within easy reach, and nothing to do but put the tea a-drawing! Notwithstanding all that has been said by former tourists, the tea was excellent, and produced no disagreeable effects. We afterwards utilized several of the geysers by boiling meat, dirty clothes, beans, coffee, etc., each experiment being attended with satisfaction. For boiled beans, two quarts of "navies" were put in a flour sack, and with a rope lowered into the steaming crater. In thirty minutes they were perfectly soft and palatable. This is not a first rate method to make allopathic bean soup, but for a homeopathic dose it can't be beat. In this connection, a little incident. Prince Telegraph's wardrobe, like our saddle-seat, was constantly getting out of repair; and as he had failed in trying to sew on a patch with a needle-gun, he was obliged

"To wear his long-tailed coat
All buttoned down before,"

(like "old Grimes,") or procure assistance. He finally compromised affairs by a change of duties: Woodall, an expert, was to sew on the patch while

Prince Telegraph washed the dishes, his first attempt probably in a lifetime. Hesitating a moment, a brilliant idea struck him. Fifty or sixty feet distant was a very noisy little geyser, with its aperture in the centre of a shallow, well-rimmed basin of about two and a half by four feet diameter, the water scarcely ever covering the flat bottom at a greater depth than two inches. Pitching the soiled tinware, knives, forks, towels, etc., into a champagne basket, and with an "Oh, no! I guess I can't wash dishes!" the Prince approaching his improvised dish-pan, unceremoniously dumped them in to soak while he placidly enjoyed his meershaum. Suddenly, and as if resenting the insult to its dignity, the little spouter spit the basin full to overflowing in a second, setting the contents in a perfect whirl, and the next instant, drawing in its breath, commenced sucking everything toward the aperture. We at the camp heard an agonizing cry for help, and looking out, beheld the Prince, with hat off and eyes peeled, dancing around his dish-pan in a frantic attempt to save the fast-disappearing culinary outfit. It was comical in the extreme. There would be a plunge of the hand in the boiling water, a yell of pain, and out would come a spoon; another plunge and yell, and a tin plate; an "Oh! ah! o-o-o!—e-e-e!" and a fork. As we arrived, the towel and one tin plate were just going out of sight; while the Prince, gazing at his parboiled hands, was profanely discussing the idea of being "sucked in" by a geyser!

As this letter already promises to be a lengthy one, only a brief description of some of the more prominent geysers will be given before bidding adieu to the basin and crossing over the divide to the Yellowstone.

In our opinion, there is no geyser in the entire region that is so richly deserving of mention as our ancient-looking, steadfast friend, Old Faithful, for its operations are as regular as clock-work, of most frequent occurrence, and of great power. Standing sentinel-like on the upper outskirts of the valley, at regular intervals of sixty-seven minutes the grim old vidette sounds forth his "All's well" in a column of water five or six feet in diameter, throwing it skyward to a distance of one hundred and fifty feet, and holding it up to that height for eight or ten minutes' duration. The stream is nearly vertical, and in descending the water forms a glittering shower of pearldrops, plashing into a succession of porcelain-lined reservoirs of every conceivable shape and of many-color tints. The mound is not far from twenty feet in height, and gradually slopes down to the south in regular terraces to a neighboring hot spring. One of the artistic reservoirs nearest the crater is half filled with irregularly-shaped, perfectly polished white pebbles, which must have been thrown out at the different eruptions. When the eruption ceases, the water recedes, and nothing is heard but the occasional escape of steam, until another exhibition occurs. "Old Faithful" will ever be the favorite of tourists, as it never fails in regularly giving a display of its powers.

Crossing the river, and proceeding down its east bank an eighth of a mile, one comes upon a very modest-appearing formation of silica, strongly resembling an old-fashioned straw beehive with the apex evenly cut off. The cone springs up from a flat crust to a height of four feet, and has an oval crater of two by three feet. It was not until the second day after arrival that our curiosity was gratified by seeing this geyser give its display. In the middle of the afternoon, without a moment's warning, the eruption took place. The column of water ejected filled the full size of the crater, and was shot up fully two hundred feet. So nearly vertical does the stream ascend, that on a calm day nine-tenths of the volume would fall directly back into the aperture. From this cause, probably, there is no mound of any con-

THE GIANTESS.

sequence built around it. At the time we witnessed its action, the ascending torrent was interposed between us and a bright shining sun, and through its cloud of spray there formed a rainbow of magnificent proportions, lending the fountain a crowning splendor and glory that it did not otherwise possess. Its period of eruption is from eight to ten minutes. From Prof. Hayden's Report, we have reason to believe that the duration of action is different at different times, as he records a convulsion of eighteen minutes.

To the right, and down stream a few hundred yards from the Beehive, is the Giantess, with a crater eighteen by twenty-five feet, scalloped and carved after the manner of the hot spring formations already described. At first inspection one hardly supposes it to be anything more than a huge degenerating spring, that, having exhausted itself by continuous overflow, was now dying out. We came upon it during one of its lucid intervals, and looking down into the gaping chasm, could just discern the water a great distance below us in a state of apparent tranquillity. Presently, however, there came up from its gloomy depths a dismal groan, quickly followed by a dense volume of steam and a rumbling sound beneath our feet, as of terrific underground thunder. In a moment more, the seething elements below were in wildest commotion. The rolling and clashing of waves; the dread, terrible rushing of steam-clouds to and fro under the frail crust; the thunder of the raging waters, as lashed into fury by the pursuing steam they sought to burst apart their prison walls and escape, all were but too distinctly heard and felt. Spell-bound we stood, and with enraptured awe silently awaited the result of this terrible confusion. Spasm succeeded spasm, the agitated flood boiled up to the surface of the crater, then with a deafening report the immense body of water was hurled into the air over one hundred feet.

Like some gigantic fountain impelled by an engine power that could have revolved a world, the boiling jet continued to play for several minutes. Surrounding this majestic liquid dome is a circle of smaller jets, issuing from the same crater but from lesser apertures below, giving the main column the appearance of a fountain within a fountain. Playing hither and thither in the mellow sunlit mist, miniature rainbows are seen, and the air glistens with the falling water-beads as if a shower of diamonds was being poured from the golden gates of the Eternal City. The Giantess, with all her grandeur and eloquence, failed to "captivate our susceptible Associate," (as hinted by our Senior when writing up our departure from Virginia,) for we had become infatuated with our damp little fairy guide, and could witness the old lady's multitude of tears without a reciprocating sigh or a desire to fall into her embrace.

On the other side of the river, about one mile further down, is the Grotto, situated on a large mound of pure white, and encircled by a cluster of hot springs. Its crater base rises some twenty feet above the mound, and is wrought into the most wonderful formation in the basin. We have seen sea-shells that came nearer bearing a resemblance to it than does anything else we think of; but as a comprehensive description cannot be given without the aid of engravers' tools, we shall attempt none. The unique formation is its greatest attraction, as its eruptions are irregular, and its force when spouting greatly inferior to any of the geysers mentioned.

Directly to the east, and quite near the river, stands haughtily out from its beautifully incrusted mound the king of the basin, known as the Giant, which, though closely watching during daylight, we did not observe in eruption. The formation is like that of a monster hollow tree with the upper portion broken off by wind. Mr. Langford says of it: "The Giant has a rugged crater, ten feet in diameter on

CATFISH GEYSER.

THE GIANT GEYSER.

the outside, with an irregular orifice five or six feet in diameter. It discharges a vast body of water, and the only time we saw it in eruption the flow of water in a column five feet in diameter and one hundred and forty feet in vertical height, continued uninterruptedly for *three hours*. The crater resembles a miniature model of the Coliseum."

Our party were interestedly inspecting the Giant and a small geyser close by, which was continually in eruption, and made as much fuss over its twenty-feet stream as if it thought itself the only spouter in the basin, and the National Park had been reserved on purpose for it to "ebulish" in, when just below us, from the opposite bank of the river, a vast column of steam burst forth and ascended several hundred feet. On the *qui vive* for new wonders, we hurried over a slight knoll in that direction, and arrived just in time to witness the Fan Geyser getting up steam for an eruption. It requires more inside machinery to operate this geyser than any of the others. In fact, it is a massive natural engine twenty-five by one hundred feet, with two small valves, two large escape pipes, and at the extreme upper end a huge smoke-stack—five separate and distinct craters.

When we arrived we could hear a sound as of throwing cord-wood into a mammoth furnace. This continued several seconds, ceased, and was followed by great quantities of steam from the smoke-stack; then the two valves opened, shooting out swift, hissing jets of steam. The next moment there would be an unearthly roar from the double crater, both would fill, and from each aperture a column of water two feet in diameter shoot upwards over eighty feet— one ascending nearly vertical, and the other at an angle of about forty-five degrees, thus forming the "fan." The eruption would continue from two to four minutes, then the flow cease for eight or ten seconds, and then the entire movement would be repeated. These repetitions continued twenty or twenty-five minutes, and then ceased altogether. It requires no great flight of fancy to see in this marvellous natural mechanism a vast engine running under the guidance of a ghostly engineer, and being "stoked" from Pluto's wood-pile by a thousand goblin firemen! Its action was watched with intense interest and delight by our party, and when the grand explosion occurred, Mr. Hillhouse Raymond seemed perfectly overcome by the exciting spectacle. Springing from the ground, he leaped into the river, waded water almost waist-deep to the opposite side, and rushing under the sparkling shower, waved his hat and shouted "Hurrah!" till out of breath. This incident is cited only for the purpose of demonstrating how grandly, delightfully impressive are these most wonderful displays. It is said of Prof. Hayden—a man of extremely nervous temperament and with an unbounded enthusiasm for the sciences—that he cannot compose himself in presence of a geyser in eruption; but, losing recollection of the material world for the time, rubs his hands, shouts, and dances around the object of his admiration in a paroxysm of gleeful excitement.

TAKING LEAVE. Besides those already mentioned, there are many other spouting geysers, each one with its own peculiar beauty and characteristics; but enough has been described, it is hoped, to give our readers a tolerably clear impression of their nature, beauty, and unapproachable grandeur. There has been no attempt on our part to exaggerate the facts in their relation, and our only regret is that no human mind, paint them in the choicest words it may, can do them justice.

We have been asked by many if there is no danger attendant upon an inspection of these curiosities. We reply, Yes; and the greatest caution should be used in leading and riding horses over the crust; in getting too near mud geysers; in remaining too near

SECOND CAÑON, YELLOWSTONE RIVER.

a geyser in eruption, (for the water is scalding hot.) There is said to be "no danger" in viewing Niagara; but scarcely a "season" is passed there that some fearful, fatal accident does not occur—and there is a hundred times more need of caution at the Geysers than at Niagara. Danger from Indians there is none. Our party stood no guard, night or day, and found no evidence of their having visited the country for years. It is said that there exists among them an unconquerable superstition that the great Manitou here displays his anger towards his red children. They avoid the region of the National Park, and only pass through it when compelled by untoward circumstances. There is another tradition current among the Sioux and Crows to this effect: Some years ago, the Sioux and Crows, then friendly to each other, were *en route* to the Upper Yellowstone and Madison rivers, on a hunting expedition; and while encamped in the second cañon of the Yellowstone, nearly opposite Emigrant Peak, they were hemmed in at both entrances by the Nez Perces, Bannachs, and Flatheads, (then, as now, at war with the Sioux and Crows,) and the whole party massacred. For this reason these tribes never ascend the river above the cañon named, for fear of meeting a similar fate.

That this and other portions of the National Park will attract the wonder-seeking tourists of the world, we have not the slightest doubt; that in a world abounding in the marvellous, the Geyser region excels any other known to civilization, needs only a personal inspection and a recourse to history to convince the most skeptical.

We now take our leave of the Geysers, and in our concluding letters shall note our visit to the Lake, Falls, and Grand Cañon of the famed Yellowstone: Tower Falls, Sulphur Mountain, and White Sulphur Springs on Gardiner river.

LETTER NO. IV.

It was the intention on leaving the Geysers to continue on up the Madison to Madison lake, strike Stevenson's trail, and cross over to Yellowstone lake—a distance of fifteen miles; but somehow we failed to follow the indistinct trail, were continually getting out of the way, and after getting on up the river five or six miles, it was determined to turn back and go *via* the lower basin. Perhaps a little experience in crossing the Madison above the Geysers, had some weight in this decision. Its recital would furnish the best of serio-comic illustrations of what unresurrected humanity can endure without profanity; but it would also put our friend Largey before the public in wet breeches, Mills on a bucking horse, Freeler "in solution," and the rest of the party in a fit of immoderate laughter; therefore we respectfully omit it.

The journey back to Lower Basin was accomplished without incident worthy of note, and on the evening of the 12th we took possession of an old camp at the foot of the range just as a huge black bear, within plain sight, made a lumbering scramble out of it at a sort of "Come where my love lies dreaming" gait. We plead Artemus Ward's excuse for not following him, and concluded that a misunderstanding with a full-grown bear is not one of the felicities to be hankered after. The experience of this camp served only to teach us how sweetly one can sleep in the middle of a three-in-a-bed lay-out when the two outsiders are pulling clothes, and how one will endure solitude to gobble more than his rightful share of the whiskey; but we don't care to recite it in detail, as our silence was purchased on the spot by an untimed draught from the stolen jug.

Bright and early next morning we took up our line of march toward the Yellowstone, twenty-four miles distant; and now, while we are watching with straining eyes to catch a last glimpse of the monarchs of Geyserland, before climbing over the divide, let us indulge in a comparison. The civilized world has for years read of the wonderful Geysers of Iceland. Historians and tourists have trumpeted their fame in oft-repeated story; every schoolboy's geography contains an account of their magnitude, and the curiosity-seeking tourists of the Old World have for nearly two centuries visited them yearly. Do not be incredulous or astonished, then, when we make the assertion—based on the most reliable scientific authorities—that these world-renowned Iceland Geysers, when compared to those within the bounds of the National Park, dwindle into utter insignificance—are the merest pigmies! In fact, there are *only two* spouting geysers in the entire Icelandic region, of sufficient importance to bear a comparison. These two are called the "Great Geyser" and the "Great Strokr." The most miraculous that is recorded of either of them is " a cone twenty feet high, aperture five feet diameter, and throwing a stream five feet in diameter a vertical height of seventy-eight feet for the space of five to seven minutes." The others are too insignificant to be mentioned. The Geysers of California, forty miles from Napa City, have also been talked of and written about for years as a sight worth travelling thousands of miles to behold. What are they? simply a few boiling springs, the like of which are so plentiful on the Madison that were fifty of them to be removed they would scarcely be missed from the magnificent collection. It is no less than a misnomer to name them geysers, and is only done in contradistinction to those springs which have no ebullition at all. The most prominent in

2*

the Napa county cluster, is recorded as having a *squirt* of fifteen feet; yet, in California, are they considered wonderful.

Suppose, for the sake of a better contrast, that we now view each of the Madison Geysers during its most violent spasm, (taking Professor Hayden's record of heights and our own observations as being correct.) First, view Old Faithful yonder, sending up its beautiful jet of six feet diameter one hundred and fifty feet skyward; look at that veritable lake of hot water, eighteen by twenty-five feet, rising into the air to a height of two hundred feet from the magnificently ornamented crater of the Giantess! Watch how her royal consort, the Giant, recognizes the summons, and with matchless grandeur replies with a stream five feet in diameter thrown one hundred and forty feet toward the stars, continually for *three hours*. See the demure-looking Bee Hive join in the revel with its splendid column of two hundred feet in height; cast your eye toward the rugged old Castle, for it is chiming in with its immaculate fount of eighty feet height and fully eight feet in diameter! now at the indescribably unique Grotto, whose boiling flood seethes forth above the tallest pines. And then, as we bid them a reluctant farewell, watch for an instant that gigantic natural engine, the Fan, getting ready to eclipse its proud rivals. Up goes the steam column from its smoke-stack, "fize-e-e, fiz-e-e!" hiss the two fierce little valves, and then with a detonation that sounds far and wide, there ascends its twin founts one hundred and fifty feet above the double crater! Can the world elsewhere furnish a scene of such surpassing grandeur? The trail across the mountain to Yellowstone, leads first through a thick brushwood, and considerably out of the way, to avoid an extensive and almost impassable swamp; then wiggles its way through a density of young pines and over much fallen timber up a heavy mountain; across a barren, sage-brush plain—and, finally, curling itself over a succession of small, well-grassed and watered valleys and meadows, leads out on the river near a cluster of mud volcanoes. After striking the river, our party moved up stream about one-half a mile, camping a distance of six miles from the lower end of Yellowstone lake the same evening. This jaunt from the lower geysers is a distance of twenty-four miles, and uses up the best part of a day, We therefore postponed our visit to Yellowstone lake until the day following. The Yellowstone is the largest and longest tributary of the Missouri, rises in the Yellowstone mountains, near the source of the Madison, in the vicinity of Sublete's lake, and is one thousand miles in length. The lake is situated in a vast depression, or basin, one hundred and twenty-five miles down stream, and is, perhaps, the most remarkable inland sea known to history. Our visit was so briefly enjoyed that we have no hope of doing its description justice, did we attempt to enter upon minutiæ. The fact of so large a body of water sleeping so beautifully calm and transparent within its circle of snow-crested mountains, at an altitude of eight thousand feet above the sea, (two thousand feet higher than Virginia City,) is wonderful in itself—and there is room for doubt that its parallel is in either hemisphere. Its western and northern shores are pebbly beaches like those of the great lakes. Fringed everywhere by its beautiful evergreens, with the cold gray mountains of the Yellowstone range mirroring their hoary crowns in its wealth of blue, the scene is picturesque and pretty. And as we delightedly watched the gently plashing wavelets kissing the pebbly strand, they seemed like troops of merry, winsome maidens coquettishly romping to challenge the admiration of the passers-by. The otherwise drowsy expanse of water is relieved of its monotony by heavily-wooded islands nestling here and there on its broad bosom, and at different points along the northeastern shore, clouds of steam are seen floating lazily upward from numerous hot springs. We can only imagine how exquisitely interesting it would be for a party of tourists in a light sailing craft or small steamer, to make a voyage of exploration to the many green isles, boiling springs and mud volcanoes; but we hope the time will not be long deferred when one can really enjoy the pleasures of such a romantic cruise.

The lake is recorded by Professor Hayden and Captain Stevenson—the latter of whom quite thoroughly explored it last year in a canvas boat—as being twenty-two miles from north to south, an average of ten to fifteen miles in width, with soundings of *three hundred feet!* In shape it is very unique, and has been aptly compared to the outlines of the human hand. Following its shore-line, the circumference cannot be much less than two hundred and fifty miles. It is fed by the fountain-stream of the Upper Yellowstone and the melting of the mountain-snows, and its waters are cool as ordinary spring-water. Fish abound in it, game in plentitude inhabits the surrounding forest, and its placid surface and grassy margins render it the earthly Paradise of a myriad of water-fowl.

The largest of the islands is Stevenson Island, and the following Captain Stevenson's description of it:

"On arriving at our permanent camp on the bank of the lake, but a short distance from its outlet, which forms the source of the Yellowstone river, we at once began the construction of a little boat, whose services in exploring the lake, making soundings, and visiting the different islands, etc., were of the greatest value. Over six hundred miles were travelled in this little craft while performing the services for which it was designed. One of the first and most interesting tasks which was undertaken

YELLOWSTONE LAKE.

with the boat, was by direction of Professor Hayden, to visit and explore the island nearest our camp, subsequently called Stevenson's Island, after Mr. James Stevenson, who, in company with Mr. Henry Elliott, first visited it. It was supposed by every one in that country that no white man had ever set foot upon this island, and it was not known that the natives of the country had ever ventured to explore it. Early on the morning of the ——, Messrs. Stevenson and Elliott embarked in the little boat and started for the island, which was judged to be about four miles distant. It was not their expectation to find the island inhabited, except by animals that could fly; but after about one-and-a-half hours rowing they reached the shore of the island, and to their utter astonishment the first thing that met their eyes was the track of a bear, the dimensions of which indicated one of the largest of his kind. On alighting from the boat and looking around, numerous tracks were observed of the same animal; also those of the wolf, elk, deer, rabbits, and evidences of a variety of smaller quadrupeds, such as mice, moles, etc.

"Indeed, the natural history of this island is quite equal to any of that portion of the Rocky mountains. It was our intention to explore this body of land thoroughly, but the great number of dangerous animals that appeared to infest it, and the difficulty of penetrating the dense jungle which overspread it, deterred us from making the attempt. Large pines of every species known to that region of the mountains, were abundant, and the undergrowth of every variety was almost impenetrable. We again embarked in our little canvas craft to sail around the island, which we found to be about four miles in circumference. Portions of its shores were well adapted for wild fowls, such as geese, ducks, and waders of all kinds, all of which were abundant. Before leaving the island, we landed again on the western shore, to make some examinations and to ascertain if any evidences of white men could be found. In wandering about we found a spear-head of white flint, made no doubt by some of the Indians still wandering about in this region, the only thing we found during our visit, to indicate that human beings had been there before."

It is a two hours' ride from the lake to the falls and grand cañon. These latter are and will be for ever the three great objects of interest in this portion of the National Park. Here is where the "Wonders of the *Yellowstone*" receive their crown of glory. To say that we can *describe* (literally) their grandeur and marvellous beauty, would be to assume to correctly portray the illuminated heavens, or carve out of poor, weak words the glories of the Heavenly City itself. The subject is beyond the conception of the most vivid imagination—language is inadequate to express the unapproachable picture presented—the eye only can photograph the gorgeous scene. The head of the cañon is but a short distance above the Upper Falls, and just before reaching them narrows down to a close gorge, compressing the waters into so small a passage-way that they drive through with great commotion. The first fall is only a quarter to a half mile above the lower one, and the stream dashes over a perpendicular cliff of one hundred and forty feet in height. Our nearest view of the Upper Falls was from the craggy summit of a projecting point of the mountain which forms a portion of the cañon wall a half-mile below. The view is one which, were there no Lower Falls to admire, would be a sufficient attraction to call forth abundant enthusiasm from the looker-on. But as one stands gazing at them from this rocky height, a mighty and continuous roaring of the fleeing tide can be heard directly beneath, challenging the undivided attention and admiration of the wonder-seeker.

UPPER FALL YELLOWSTONE, 140 FEET.

The river between these two great precipices is dashed into a turbulent, foamy cascade, by its ragged bed and lightning speed, and does not again become smooth until just the instant it takes its dizzying leap of *three hundred and ninety feet* perpendicularly to its narrow bed in the depths of the great cañon. On either side of the falls, and so far as the eye can reach below, there rises to a height of two thousand feet above the river, a grand, vast wall of infinite masonry so gorgeously colored and tinted, so bounteously beautified in gild, purple and carmine, that no oil-painting or chromo, however fine, will ever do justice to the natural picture! There is no painful glare of one color prominent over another: the great Artist has used each brush deftly, and with his divinely exquisite touches each tint and shade is so perfectly blended, that the mighty walls seem as if built by the equal commingling of all the precious metals of the world! The bright sunlight pours over the immense barrier with all its dazzling rays against the imprisoning walls, and reflecting from side to side, is melted into an amber flood of mellow light; while the beautiful surroundings, canopied o'er by the soft blue dome of an autumnal sky, give forth Nature's warmest, kindliest smile to her ardently worshipping children.

Clambering along the side of the steep bluff just above the falls, Messrs. Largey, Freeler, Woodhall, and the writer, successfully made the descent to the river, and stood on the very brink of the majestic cliff. Never did mortal eye behold a sight of more sublime magnificence, as within three paces of the roaring cataract we peered into the abyss below. Never did Divine ingenuity carve out a more superb frame for a more lovely river than is here before our vision. Like an immense sheet of silver foil, the waters spread out and hang tremblingly over the appalling chasm—for a moment frantically clinging to the cliff, as if afraid to trust the Deity who has marked out its weird pathway, and then reassured by an abiding faith in Him "who doeth all things well," it trustingly falls into the extended arms of the mighty cañon, far, far beneath, where it again glides onward to the great Missouri. On the very verge of the precipice, fairly peeping over at the sheet, is a thrifty little pine that has there been sown by some poetic zephyr in its frolics through the wild cañon. Reaching out, we plucked for each of our comrades a sprig and cone, as a memento of the delightful visit—a souvenir that we trust will be treasured until in the dim gold of life each one can recount to listening, youthful ears, the happy journeyings of our little party to its picturesque home by the great Falls of the Yellowstone.

CRYSTAL FALLS.

LETTER NO. V.

We do not wish the reader to infer that we esteem Yellowstone *Falls* the most majestic or grand of any yet discovered; but in many respects they are unquestionably the most beautiful and wonderful. There are others which leap from a greater height, and some that carry a much larger volume of water; but we doubt if there is another cataract in the universe that is surrounded with so great a variety of magnificent and interestingly romantic scenery. The very poetry of nature seems to have clustered itself around this its wild, unknown, and almost unheard of prodigy, wreathing into rhymes its wilderness of sentiment and music, and permeating every nook and corner of its weird surroundings with romance, harmony, and splendor. There is an irresistible, captivating mellowness and beauty in the very trees that so gorgeously fringe the gilded landscape, thickly gathered as they are on the summit of each cañon wall, peering at each other across the wild chasm between, and here and there cautiously approaching the great cascade, as if afraid of venturing too near, lest dizzy-headed they should fall into the cloud of mist below. There is an exhilarating freshness in the air, as the feathery spray bejewels each twig and leaf with its crystal dews; and the mystical music of the falling waters sings a never-ceasing legend of its eternal vigils.

We have lived long within sound of the echoings of the mighty Niagara; have gazed for hours at the mighty flood and its broad, grand sheet; loitered leisurely around its magnificent environs, and more than once—*played "freeze out" for lager* at its villainous refreshment saloons. There you have all the poetry knocked out of Niagara in less than a dozen words. And so it is in reality. The persistent blab of its "oldest inhabitant," (he is at least triplets,) who knows a deal more about them than you care to know; the hauling and swindling of its hundred dastardly, profane hack-drivers; its rattle of wagons, shrieks of locomotives, and the thought that about all the world has seen them before you, divests them of romance, if not of grandeur. Still they are the mightiest cascades in the world. The waters of four great lakes find outlet over their immense precipice, and their volume is the escaping flood of an inland ocean. But their height (one hundred and sixty-four feet) is two hundred and twenty-six feet less than our beautiful Falls of the National Park. The sheet at Niagara is eleven hundred feet in breadth, while that of the Yellowstone is less than two hundred. The discordant roar of Niagara is liquid music at Yellowstone; the majesty of the former is poetry at the latter. The waters which dash over Niagara flow through a level and monotonous region, and have a weary, business-like appearance; while the Yellowstone, gliding through a region sublime in scenery and associations everywhere, falls into the grandest cañon in the world. The former are three hundred feet above sea level; the latter, eight thousand! The great Suspension Bridge is but two hundred and fifty-eight feet above the water. A like bridge across the Grand Cañon would rise *two thousand feet* above the little stream.

In this connection, it may prove a matter of information to some of our readers to devote a few lines to mention of other great waterfalls. (We never yet saw a man that did not have a weakness for "waterfalls" of one kind or another.)

Yosemite river, in California, leaps down three perpendicular walls—two thousand sixty-three feet in all—the greatest of which is an abrupt fall of thirteen hundred feet; the second leap is two hundred and fifty, and the third four hundred and fifty feet. The stream is not so large as Yellowstone, but its inconceivable beauty, and the State Park by which it is enclosed, is the pride of California. The Canopoh falls, on the Merced, in the same state, are three hundred and fifty feet perpendicular. The Merced has already made a leap a half mile farther up stream, at what is called the Nevada falls. These are nearly three hundred and fifty feet high, but not so picturesque as those below. The Merced is thrice favored in beautiful cataracts, making a third and direct plunge over a cliff six hundred feet in height at Tusayac falls. But neither of the three will bear comparison to the lofty Yosemite, and are but little mentioned by tourists. In Montana, the great Falls of the Missouri, seventy-five miles (by river) above Fort Benton, and eighty feet in height, are eminently worthy of note, and are remarkable, if for nothing else, on account of being the only barrier to navigation of the Missouri for a distance of five thousand miles—accepting the fact that the Missouri is entitled to the name all the way to New Orleans. The Sho-sho-ne falls, on Snake river, Idaho, are two hundred feet perpendicular, and carry over a volume of water as large as the Missouri at Benton. The cataract itself is impressively grand, but the country around them, as at Niagara, is tame, and lacks the inspiriting influence of mountain scenery. In fact, the vicinity is as fully deserving of the appellation of *Les Mauvis Terres* as that which now rests under that geographical imprecation. Genesee falls, one hundred feet high, and within a stone throw of where the New York Central Railroad bridge crosses the Genesee river at Rochester, N. Y., are perhaps most noted from the thrifty commercial centre that has grown up around them, their immense utilized water power, and the fact that it was here the barbarous natives of the Flour City were wont to be amused at seeing the eccentric Sam Patch jump from the brink into what finally proved his watery and unhallowed grave.

And so we might continue to extend mention of the many notable waterfalls with which "our own America" abounds, but deem the citation of those so briefly referred to above sufficient for comparison.

We admit a partiality for scenery—are particularly so to falls, and cannot even placidly gaze upon a jauntily-arranged "waterfall" without contemplating how divinely (in this instance alone) woman's art has superceded nature in throwing around its history so many hairbreadth escapes. Thus it is, in leaving Yellowstone to be visited and admired by those who have had patience to read of our wanderings, that we venture the assertion that, with the single exception of the fall of Adam, Yellowstone furnishes more food for thought than any other we have knowledge of.

Circling around the falls is a great extent of country that is rich in beautiful streams, gigantic mountains, splendid valleys, and dense forests—in every nook, cañon, and dell of which there is much to please the eye, but we are forced to pass it with a general recommendation.

On the morning of September 16 we again broke camp, and started down the river. There are so many different trails just about the vicinity of the falls, that without a previous knowledge of the right one, the tourist is apt to become puzzled, but by keeping well out of the belt of timber next the river, there is no trouble in striking the Hayden trail. Only one incident occurred on that day worthy of reference, and we only allude to that in order to show the necessity of parties keeping well together on a trip of this kind. One of the party—Hillhouse Raymond—lingered behind to have "just one more look at the falls," promising to overtake the party "in a few minutes." The forenoon passed without his joining us, and no little concern began to be felt for his safety. Alarm increased to such an extent that it was finally determined to despatch a party in search. According, Mr. Largey and the Doctor took the back trail, spending afternoon and night in search and anxiety, the others of the party keeping on and camping at Tower falls, fifteen miles below. On reaching Tower creek, we there found a note from the missing man informing us that, having missed the trail on leaving the Falls, and failing to find us, he should ride on to Gardner river, eighteen miles from his note. While we supposed him lost, our sympathies were all with him; but knowing of his safety, thinking of the Prince and Esculapius then searching "the howling wilderness" (a hoot owl—Largey insists that it was the original whangdoodle—serenaded the searchers that night) for his remains, and the trouble his insatiable curiosity had caused, we could have seen him "held in solution" with a savage pleasure. Largey and the Doctor, who did not overtake us till the day after, probably shared our feelings.

Tower creek has its source in the lofty ridge of mountains which divide the main branch of the Missouri from the Yellowstone, of which it is a feeder. For a distance of eight or ten miles up from the latter river it flows through a deep, rugged cañon. Great bowlders and many in number obstruct the passage-way of the swift-running stream, and as it noisily glides through its gloomy cleft, it adds the most enchanting feature to a landscape of much scenic beauty. Some two hundred yards from its mouth, joyfully hailing the prospective release from its wild environs, its springs from its bed and leaps down a precipice one hundred and fifty-six feet perpendicular, dashing itself into foam on the rocks below. These falls are delightful, and a descent to the bottom of the gorge, where the finest view of the sheet is obtained, well repays the trouble of getting down. Around the falls, on each side of the cañon, immense spires or pinnacles rise up grim and black, giving the place an architectural air, as if it had once been the site of some lordly castle whose glory had been obliterated by the ravages of time. Although of course immovable, some of the monster towers seem as if about to topple over into the chasm, and one experiences a feeling of greater security as he again passes out from under their threatening shadows. Walking to the mouth of the creek, another fine view of the Grand Cañon is had. Here are more evidences of a sulphurous compound than at the falls. The cañon has a brighter yellow tinge, and the various stratifications of basalt are artistically equal. In various places small springs of sulphur-water ooze out from the wall, giving a strong and unpleasant odor to the vicinity. From here to White Mountain Hot-Springs it is eighteen miles, and for the greater part of the way the trail is tolerably good, with hill-climbing enough to satisfy the stoutest-limbed adventurer. We got a late start from Tower creek, took the day leisurely, and arrived at the springs just as twilight began deeping into dark. We have already, during our series of sketches, devoted considerable space to the description of the hot-springs of the National Park, but at the risk of wearying the reader we shall, as briefly as possible, refer to this enormous formation. White Mountain Hot-Spring is situated on Gardner's river, about seventy-five miles distant from Bozeman, and before the National Park Bill became a law, was taken possession of by two very estimable young men of Bozeman, Messrs. Horr and McCartney, in anticipation of their value as a resort for tourists and invalids. These springs are at an elevation of one thousand feet above the river, and their centuries of flowing down the mountain-side have deposited their mineral solutions from top to bottom of the slope. The mineral chiefly contained in the

GRAND CAÑON, YELLOWSTONE.

water is what is known to the analytic scientist as *calcareo-sulphurous*—a combination of lime and sulphur—but it also possesses soda, alumina, and magnesia. The formation, extending over an area not less than one mile square, is of a yellowish white; but there are portions of the hill where the deposit is white as the driven snow, and others, where sulphur predominates, yellow as gold. At the top of the hill is a group of hot-springs, some in an active state, others showing but faint signs of ebullition, and still others with nothing now remaining but the dry and pulseless crater formation. The most powerful active spring is located about the centre of the summit, is about eighteen by thirty feet in diameter, and has the same exquisite rim-decorations and ultramarine coloring inside as those of the Geyser Basin. From this spring now flows most of the water which traverses the side-hill.

At the period when this grand cluster of springs was in fullest operation the mountain must have presented a spectacle of wondrous magnificence. From the summit to its base the constant overflow and cooling of the solution from the springs above have formed a succession of gorgeous terraces. The surface of each of these terraces is covered by small, prettily-fashioned reservoirs, which receive the waters, and overflowing, delivers them again to those of the terrace next below. It would be difficult to estimate the number of these little urns, as the entire side surface of the mountain is made up of them, each one a marvel in itself. At a point one mile above, on the Tower creek trail, the formation bears a strong resemblance to an immense cascade, which in its dashing and foaming has suddenly frozen to its bed in huge, immaculate waves.

In passing downward one can bathe in any desired temperature of water, from hot to cold. There are numerous small sulphur-springs and caves in the vicinity, and but a short distance away we found a veritable geyser. It is of the second class, and now rapidly dying out. There are many other curiosities to be seen in the neighborhood of White Mountain; and if we had not determined to close our series with the present article, we could dilate to any extent on the many stalactite and stalagmite formations to be found in the vast caverns beneath the crust of the mountain; the crater formations of extinct geysers; the romantic cascades just above on Gardner river; the remarkable "Liberty Cap"—a solid cone-shaped rock fifty feet in height rising out of the first terrace of White Mountain—and the general surroundings. The water flowing from these springs is said to possess great medicinal qualities, and on that account alone they have this season been visited by scores of invalids. At the time of our visit some fifteen or twenty persons were there doing penance for past indiscretions by a glorious exile and hot-water baths three times a day.

Leaving this point, from there on to Bozeman there is little to be seen that is not common to almost any part of Montana—high mountains, level plateaus, beautiful streams, and all that contributes to her unsurpassed wealth of scenery. The distance is seventy-five miles, all of which can now (1873) be accomplished in a wagon. We arrived at Bozeman on the evening of September 20. We do not intend to tell how nicely we were treated on our arrival by the denizens of the eastern metropolis; nor how virgin stomachs fell a prey to the insinuating wiles of Mr. Hostetter's Purely Vegetable Bitters, and obliged their owners to *unload over the tongue* in the dead hour of night; nor how sorry our whole party of jolly tourists appeared to feel at the near approach of a pleasant journey's end. We shall silently pass by the manner in which friend Hillhouse, abetted by Prince Telegraph, inveigled our editorial brother of the "Northwest" and the writer into "a short cut to Cherry Creek," and the patient, even jovial com-

VOLCANIC TUFFS, YELLOWSTONE VALLEY.

placency with which the two editors followed the "short cut" takers' lead through brush and over mountain until twelve o'clock on that dark and frosty night, only to find that Raymond and Largey were lost, and we obliged to camp on the lee side of a big log. without supper, blankets, or a prospect for breakfast. But we must have the privilege of saying that we have never enjoyed a more pleasant and interesting vacation than on our rides through the National Park. There were no disagreeable bickerings in that little party of ours; each one contributed from the bright pages of his book of life that which kindled warmest friendships; mountain echoes oft told a story of song and jollity; and if there is an ugly disposition in either one of our companions, it was so completely buried beneath good humor, kind-heartedness, and the sunny side of existence, that we did not even get a glimpse of it.

In closing, we cannot help congratulating the people of Montana on holding the key of access to this most wonderful region, a region that at no distant day will attract the tourists of both continents, and direct the attention of the scientific world to our mountain land. It is an honor due to Montana alone that she, by her adventurous and enterprising people, with the aid of her delegate in Congress, has given to the National Union the only National Pleasure-ground within her boundaries—a museum of wonders so grand that the collections of the outside world combined cannot surpass it in all that is magnificent, beautiful, and interesting.

It should be a matter of satisfaction and pride to all that it has been set apart as a forever legacy to the people of the country; and now that the preliminary step has been taken, no obstacle should be thrown in the way of a munificent appropriation by Congress for the purpose of building roads to and through it, and otherwise making its visitation convenient for tourists.

Prof. Hayden deserves great credit for the able manner in which he has performed the labors of its survey and geologization, and his annual Reports will be read with much interest.

To our readers who have followed us on over the trail we can only say we hope the journey has not proven a tiresome one. And with this we spur our cayuse into town and finish our "Rides through the National Park."

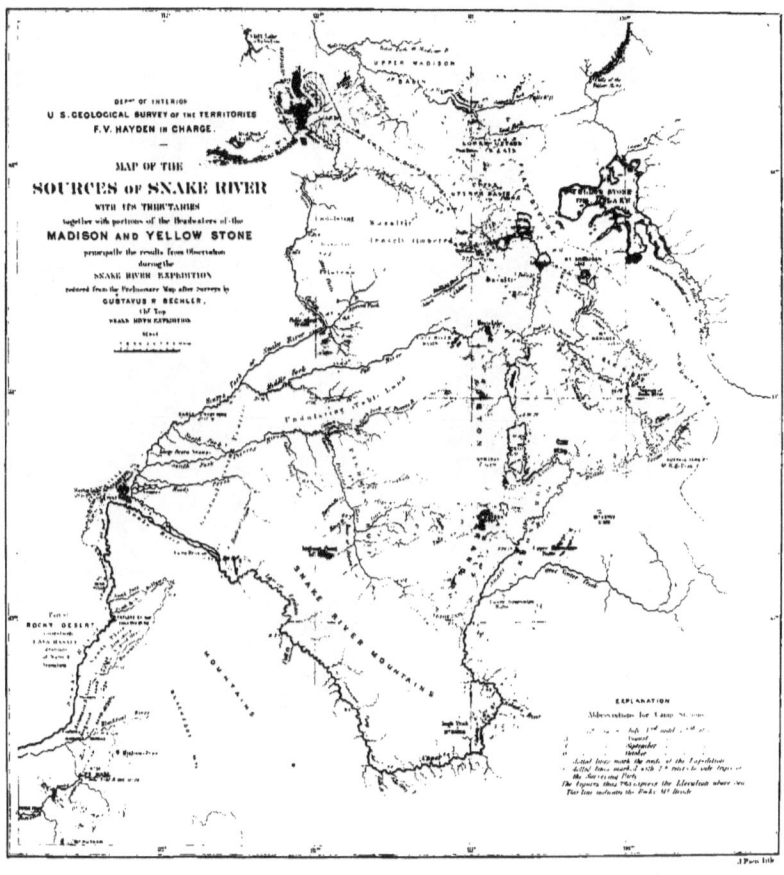

THE ROUTE OF TOURISTS

FROM THE EAST,

TO THE NATIONAL PARK,

Is over any of the connecting lines of railway to Omaha, Nebraska; thence over the Union and Central Pacific Railroads to Corinne, Utah; thence by Gilmer & Salisbury's Overland Coaches (no railroad at present) to Virginia City, Montana. First-class fare from Omaha to Corinne over the Union Pacific Railroad is $79 15; second-class, (by the same train,) $63 75. Stage fare from Corinne to Virginia City, $50. Through tickets from Omaha to Virginia City, first-class, can be purchased at Omaha at $116 75—a saving of $16 75. The distance from Omaha to Corinne *via* the Union and Central Pacific is 1,055 miles; and from Corinne *via* Gilmer & Salisbury's Overland Stage Line to Virginia City, 380 miles: time, three days.

This route is by far the quickest at the present time. The scenery along the Union Pacific Railroad is in many places very fine, the management of the road and its passenger accommodations superb, and the journey one easily made and full of interest. (For minute description of scenery, etc., etc., see Crofutt's Tourist's Guide.) The three hundred and eighty miles of stage travel, which at first thought seems tedious, is made over a splendid road, in fine, commodious four and six horse Concord coaches, which are run through from Corinne to Virginia City in three days. The meal stations along the route are first-class, and travellers receive every accommodation and comfort possible.

The second route from the East is *via* the Northern Pacific Railroad to Bismarck, Missouri river; thence by steamer up the Yellowstone to the junction of the stage and wagon road to Bozeman, Montana. This line is not yet (October 1, 1873) established the entire distance through, but it will be in the near future. This route is also pleasant in scenery, and when completed will be much the shortest and quickest route from the East to the Park.

The third route is *via* the Northern Pacific Railroad to Bismarck; thence up the Missouri river by steamer to Fort Benton, Montana; thence by Gilmer & Salisbury's stage line to Helena, Montana, (distance one hundred and forty miles;) and thence by stage to Virginia City or Bozeman.

There is but one route from the West; and that from all points in California and Nevada *via* the Central Pacific Railroad to Corinne, Utah; and thence over the stage line mentioned above, to Virginia City.

The tourist has a choice of starting points: one from Virginia City over the Grand Rounds to Bozeman; and from Bozeman over the Grand Rounds to Virginia City. Both routes are given, and each is equally recommended.

ROUTE FROM VIRGINIA CITY, MONTANA.

The tourist starting from Virginia City for the Geyser Basins is afforded two routes, both attractive in scenery and the many opportunities for hunting and fishing afforded. One is *via* the Horseback Trail up the Madison river; the other, and by far the quickest, easiest, and best, is over the VIRGINIA CITY AND NATIONAL PARK FREE WAGON ROAD, now completed through to the Upper Geyser Basin, a distance of ninety-five miles. The wagon road commences at the southeast limit of the city, and follows over the foot-hills *via* a cluster of beautiful mountain lakes, five miles distant, striking the Madison river at Wigwam creek, fourteen miles from Virginia City. At a distance of half a mile from Wigwam creek it crosses the Madison, and follows the stream to a point just above the crossing of Lawrence creek. Here it recrosses the Madison to the west bank, and closely follows the river to Big Bend, or to what is perhaps better known as Driftwood, three miles below the second cañon of the Madison. From Driftwood the road, leaving the river to the left, follows through an easy pass for a distance of eighteen miles to Lake Henry, the head-water of Henry's Fork of the Snake river. From Virginia City to Henry's lake is a distance of sixty miles—an easy day and a half ride or drive.

Henry's lake is the most prominent point of interest on the road between Virginia City and the Geyser Basins, and deserves more than a passing notice. As we have said, it is one of the main feeders of the Snake river, and is sixty-four hundred and forty-three feet above the level of the sea. The lake is five miles in length by three in breadth, and its waters abound in salmon-trout, and other fine varieties of the finny tribes. The marshy flats surrounding furnish a breeding-place and habitation for myriads of water-fowl; and ducks of many varieties, geese, gray and white swan, pelican, crane, and cormorant can be here killed almost without limit. Mr. Gilman Sawtelle, an old and well-known hunter and trapper, is the proprietor of this beautiful place, and has built a substantial and commodious house of accommodation for the convenience of tourists. He has been here since 1866, living almost wholly by the capture of fish and game, and their sale in the Virginia City market. His annual "catch" of trout is nearly forty thousand fish, and the number of elk, deer, antelope, moose, and bear slaughtered will reach nearly four hundred head yearly. A gentleman of refined tastes and more than ordinary culture, with a thorough knowledge and appreciation of the grand scenery in the midst of which he is situated, tourists will find his acquaintance and guidance beneficial and entertaining. To the south of the lake is Sawtelle's Peak, and to the west, Red Rock lake, while in the distance looms up into the clouds the Three Tetons. The view is grand and interesting, and tourists will very naturally wish to stop at the lake at least one day.

From Sawtelle's ranchero the road plainly follows down the east shore of the lake for three miles in a southerly direction; then veers to the northeast, passes through Targee Pass, (altitude seven thousand and sixty-three feet,) down Beaver Dam creek, over the south fork of the Madison, and at a distance of eighteen miles from the lake strikes the mouth of the Fire-Hole cañon, sixteen miles from the lower Geyser Basin; thence through the cañon, crossing the river twice, and following it closely to the basin.

Tourists travelling on horseback from Virginia City, and not desiring to go *via* Henry's lake, can either follow the wagon road to Driftwood, or keep along the west bank of the Madison the entire distance. The camping places, with good wood, water, and grass, are abundant all the way, and to specify in these general directions each creek and camping place would but serve to confuse the tourist.

From Big Bend or Driftwood the horseback trail continues up the right bank of the river, and where the country becomes open and rolling to the right, is indistinct in some places. Follow near the river to the mouth of the cañon. About two hundred yards below the mouth of the cañon, just below the timber, and where a little stream puts in, there is a practicable ford, somewhat swift and rocky, as all the river is below the cañon, but not very deep. Head a little up stream to centre, and then go square across. It is fifty-five or sixty miles from Virginia City to the mouth of the cañon.

The camp at the mouth of the cañon is not good; cold draught, wood distant, and feed poor. If you have time, go up the cañon about four miles, when you reach a little mountain-encircled valley, where has been an old Indian camp. It is a gorgeous place. Before reaching it, two or three cascades, far up the mountain to the left, foaming down a thousand feet, and disappearing, will please your fancy. The cañon is about six miles long; scenery fine.

On leaving the old Indian camp, the trail makes an abrupt angle to the right, and as you make the exit into the Madison basin, every characteristic of river and scene changes from the wild, rugged, and grand, to luxuriantly-grassed low-lands, a placid river, and little tributaries, deep, tranquil, and shored like those you read about in the Bible before you left the States. There is fine trouting in the larger of these. This basin is nearly circular, having a diameter of twenty-five to forty miles.

On approaching a point nearly opposite an isolated mountain standing out in the valley, you leave a considerable little stream—where you should camp, unless you have four hours daylight ahead—and on leaving it strike a little belt of swamp. Work across the swamp in the general direction you have been travelling. You will strike the plain trail on the higher ground ahead. It leads along about parallel with the left base of the mountains, and a couple of miles distant. Six or eight miles onward the trail enters the timber, which extends from there up to the mouth of the Upper Cañon. Two or three miles farther on, the trail comes out on the river. The trail is indistinct in this timber, and small fallen trees frequently obstruct progress. On reaching the river, camp under the bluff, and graze horses above.

If in doubt at any time, you can reach the river by bearing off to the right a short distance, and follow up near the stream; good travelling. If lost, or wishing to save distance, instead of following the tortuous river, head for a point a mile to right of the mouth of the cañon, which is in sight directly ahead on the general direction of the trail from the time you enter the basin. There is a good camp a couple of miles below the cañon.

The basin is a paradise for fish and water-fowl, and the surrounding valley and forests the home and grazing-place of antelope, deer. elk, and other four-footed game. The distance through this basin is about thirty miles to the upper cañon. The river here plunges into and through a deep and rugged cañon of eight miles in length, the trail leading in and out of the river several times. The scenery is fine, with stupendous and impressive cliffs and immense walls of bare brown rock. The trail leads the tourist safely out of the cañon and to the crossing of the east fork of the Fire-Hole, where is a splendid camping place; water, grass, and fish abundant.

A trip up the East Fork will be found interesting, as along it and near its head is a fine cluster of hot, boiling, and sulphur springs, ornamental basins, extinct geysers, etc., where some of the very prettiest and most curious specimens of crystals of sulphur may be obtained. From the camp at the crossing to these curiosities and return, the trip can be made in six hours, and will well repay the time. After crossing the East Fork, the trail zigzags up the ridge, having a general bearing to the right, with timber all the way to the Fire-Hole, which is reached in an hour's ride. Soon after reaching the stream you pass a handsome cascade of thirty or forty feet fall, with a miniature island just above. Here will be found a tolerable good camp for a small party, with grazing along the stream and on the island. If there is two hours of daylight ahead, however, the tourist will continue on to the lower Geyser Basin before camping.

At a little distance above the island the horseback trail again intersects the wagon road, which of course will be followed into the first Geyser Basin. The picturesque little cascades and island are still without names. Admire them, name them after your sister, wife, or sweetheart, and pass on up the river four miles farther to the lower Geyser Basin, where you get your first glimpse of hot water in a large cone-shaped mound just at the edge of the timber. The trail keeps around to the left of this, and within a few hundred yards leads to a beautiful white sulphur spring, reposing like an immense sea-shell in the river's edge. Do not become too long fascinated with its handsome fount, for there are greater marvels ahead. Follow the trail a half mile farther on, finding a muttering, sputtering mud caldron nestled under the base of the hill, and having for its immediate companions great basins of white, soft, boiling paint. Careful now lest your horse stumble and throw you into the seething pool of paint, whence egress will be difficult for man or beast. Hot springs are now abundant—to the right of you, to the left of you, and all around you. You will speed several hours in their inspection, and think each one as visited prettier than the one you have just left. These springs vary in temperature from 115 degrees to 210 degrees. Following up stream a half mile farther, through a succession of these springs, with here and there a second-class geyser, you will find a good camping place in an isolated grove of pines close to the river bank. Picket the horses, and camp in the grove during your stay in the lower basin.

All of the points of interest can now be easily visited on foot. You will want ducks for supper, and will find them on the back track and to the left one half mile, in a little marshy-shored lake almost hidden from view by the cluster of trees which surround it.

3*

The trees render the approach covered, and nine times out of ten you will get a good shot at ducks or geese. To the left of your camp, on a white eminence, three-fourths of a mile away, is the main cluster of hot springs and active geysers, from the overflow of which many tiny hot-water rivers are trickling toward the main stream.

At the extreme upper end of this eminence is Thud Geyser, so named from the dull, suppressed sound which is given as the water rises and recedes. It has a beautifully shaped rim, and around the orifice is a cluster of small basins holding water at a temperature of 185°.

Keeping on to the south of these, passing numerous small geysers and springs, all curious, you reach Fissure Spring, an oblong aperture, four by forty feet, with water scalding hot and clear as crystal; temperature 175°. Near this is a boiling lake fifty feet in diameter, with many apertures, some of which throw a continuous jet to the height of thirty feet.

South of Thud Geyser is Fountain Geyser, a huge basin of one hundred and fifty feet diameter, and a crater within the rim of twenty-five feet diameter. From this crater in the middle of the basin the entire mass of boiling water is thrown up fifty to sixty feet in height, falling back into it in detached globules like molten silver. There is an elegantly carved rim around the inner crater three feet high, and during an eruption the representation of a beautiful fountain is most natural.

A short distance still south is the famous Chalk Vat, forty by sixty feet in diameter. This is so thoroughly described in the Horseback Rides that we omit it here.

One-fourth of a mile west from the Chalk Vat are some extensive fissure springs, one of them one hundred feet in length, and varying in width from four to six feet. Many of these springs seem to remain full to the rim of the crater, and in a state of

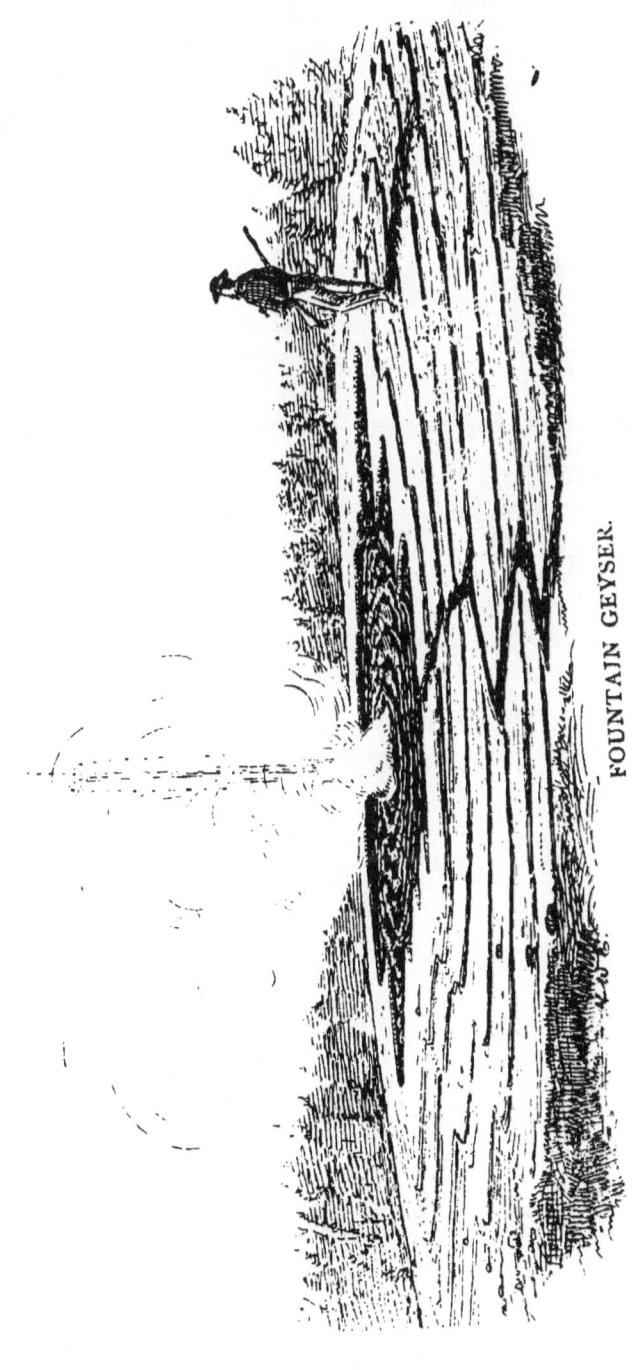

FOUNTAIN GEYSER.

continual ebullition, and yet no water flows from them. Others discharge great quantities of steam and water. Many of them deposit a curious black sediment, like fine gunpowder, and send forth a very disagreeable odor.

On the southeast side of the basin is another large group of springs, similar to those already mentioned, which should not be missed by the tourist. The jaunt is inconsiderable and the wonders numerous. This group includes some of the largest size, and the rim and crater decorations are unsurpassed by any yet seen. The colors are of brightest pink and rose, from the oxide of iron contained in the waters. Some of these are veritable geysers, and send up their jets to the height of ten to twenty feet. The aggregated waters from this cluster flow down with considerable rapidity toward the Fire-Hole river over steps and terraces, each step and terrace holding a tiny pool, and thus on step by step to the river beyond. The luxuriant growth of hot water vegetation in and along the borders of the little terraces and streams are a wonder of beauty. The channel of one is carpeted with a yellowish-pink plant, bordered by a green, silky fringe, and as this bed of fringe-bordered leaves vibrate with the shining ripples, the senses are deceived, and they seem but the magical growth of flowers of fairy-land.

In the lower portion of the group last referred to is the Architectural Fountain, an elegantly scalloped, nearly circular basin, twenty feet in diameter, with vertical sides to an unknown depth. The entire mass of water is at times most violently agitated, and overflowing the rim, passes off into terraced pools or reservoirs to the main stream, producing some of the most fantastic architecture ever seen. The color is brilliant and pleasing to the eye, and the structure a marvellous piece of natural imagery.

Near the Architectural Fountain is the White Dome, with an elevated and oddly-shaped chimney.

It has at one time been a geyser of considerable power, as the overflow has formed a broad mound of fifteen feet in height, out of which rises a chimney twenty feet high. There is a steady issue of steam from its orifice, but little water is thrown out.

There are very many attractions in the lower basin, which the casual eye of the tourist would not detect without direction. Let the tourist, then, ascend Twin Buttes, on the west side of the basin, and take a bird's-eye view of the valley below him. The summit of these buttes are six hundred and thirty feet above the Fire-Hole river, and for twenty miles up and down the stream the view is sublime. Trickling down the mountain side, directly opposite the buttes, are numerous small cascades. Here a beautiful placid lake is quietly sleeping on the very crest of the mountain, and over to the right of your lofty position is something you would have never discovered but for the ascent. It is the Fairy's Fall, the graceful beauty of which cannot be surpassed in the universe. Its volume of water is so tiny and delicate, that as you first behold it, it seems like a ribbon of white satin shining through its green and trembling veil of evergreen bows by which the cliff is surrounded. This bright little stream drops down a clear descent of two hundred and fifty feet, falling into a rocky basin at the foot of the precipice.

After viewing the beauties and marvels of the lower basin to your heart's content, descend the buttes to camp, and if you have three hours of the day left, pack up and proceed on your way to the upper or Grand Geyser Basin, nine miles distant, directly up the Fire-Hole river. There are two trails for a part of the way; one leading out on the foothills and through considerable fallen timber, and the other following close to the river bank. There is little difference; take your choice and push ahead, keeping your patience as far from the fingers' ends as possible, for this part of the journey will try it.

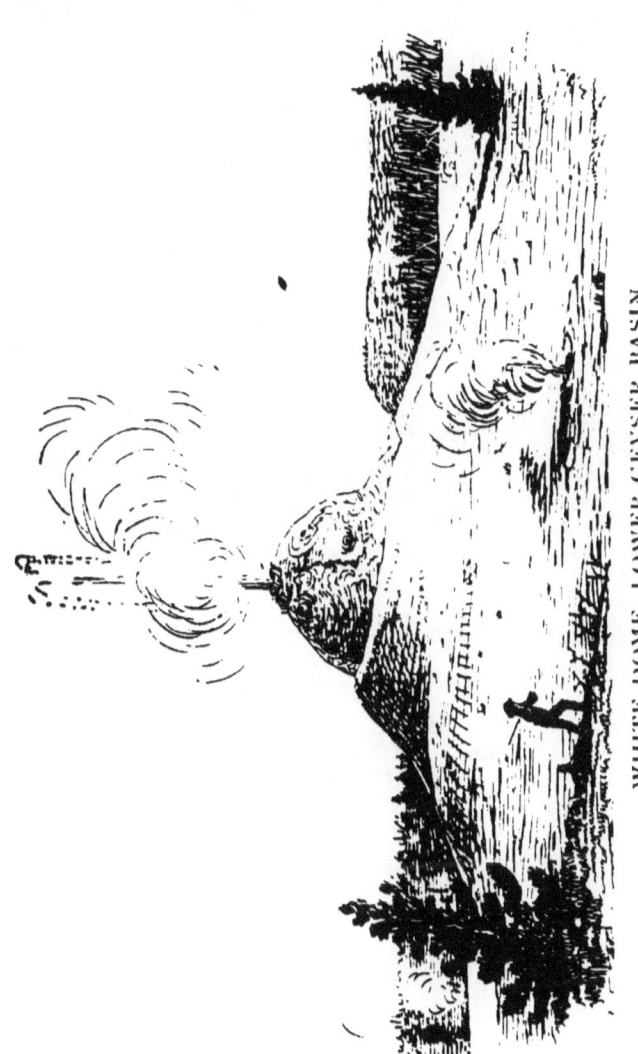

WHITE DOME, LOWER GEYSER BASIN.

After you leave the lower basin, taking the river trail along the left bank, at a distance of three miles, you will notice upon the opposite bank a tremendous overflow of hot water running into the river. This is occasioned by an enormous hot spring some two hundred yards from the river, and for a distance of one thousand yards the river bank has been gorgeously colored and decorated by the mineral sediment. This grand spring can only be fairly appreciated by being seen. Dr. Hayden has most appropriately named it the Great Spring, and it certainly is the grandest hot spring ever seen by human eye. It has an aperture *two hundred and fifty feet in diameter*, with surrounding walls or sides thirty feet high. The waters are in constant ebullition, and great columns of steam ever arising, fill the orifice. As a passing breeze sweeps away the steam for a moment, one looks down into this terrible seething pit with amazement and awe. The terrific is here so much more suggestive than the beautiful, that the beholder involuntarily shudders as he cautiously peers into the yawning gulf of hot water and steam, and friend clings to friend lest an unwary step or the reeling brain shall precipitate them into the frightful chasm.

Another spring is found close by which possesses its own unique characteristics, and which has been left to the christening of admiring travellers. This spring is shaped much like a funnel, is twenty feet in diameter at the top, and gradually tapers down to a small aperture far, far below. The rim and inside lining and ornamentation are marvellously beautiful, and no fairy palace of the imagination can approximate to a correct conception of the reality. Around its basin, and covering a large area, the crust is covered with a soft, impressible pulp, which yields to the tread like a cushion, and the brilliant coloring of which far surpasses that of the most exquisite tapestry carpet. This pulp or carpet is nearly two inches thick, and huge masses may be easily peeled up. It is vain, however, to endeavor to preserve it as a specimen, as when dry it is like gauze, the slightest breath of air shivering it to atoms. Above this, on the east margin of the river, are three more boiling springs worth seeing, but which need not be particularly described, as they are very similar to those just mentioned.

Leaving this last group, there are no more springs to be seen until the upper Geyser Basin is reached. On entering this grand geyser valley, suppress for the time your curiosity and admiration, and proceed on up the river for a distance of one mile. Here cross to the west bank, (the crossing is safe at any place,) and select a suitable camping place. Immediately after crossing, and a little up stream, near Castle Geyser, is a cluster of tall pines. This is a good camp for a small party. There is plenty of wood, shelter from the rain and sun, and hot and cold water within fifteen paces. There is another good camp one fourth of a mile above, on the same side of the river, in a neck of small pines, fronted by a small, well-grassed meadow, sufficient for grazing for a limited number of horses. Either camp is in plain view of nearly all the most prominent geysers. Directly back or west of Castle Geyser, through the open woods for half a mile, you will find a splendid pasture for any number of horses. It is a heavily-grassed meadow of about three miles circumference, and in the centre a cold-water lake of two hundred yards in length. This is the best place to send the horses if you wish to spend several days in the basin, as no doubt you will.

In the description of the wonders of the Upper Basin, to avoid repetition, we have omitted much that is portrayed in the Horseback Rides, being more particular in giving localities and names than in reviewing their beauty. Your camp being now so nearly the centre of the basin, it is deemed best to commence our description at the farthest point

BIRD'S-EYE VIEW, UPPER GEYSER BASIN.

up, and following down stream, give the location and names of the prominent geysers on either side of the river. First in order, then, standing at the extreme upper end of the basin, on the west side of the river, is Old Faithful, which will ever be the favorite of tourists. Old Faithful is so named from its regular intervals of eruption. Once every sixty-seven minutes, without fail, it gives its grand exhibition, and one can as confidently expect its display as he does the hands of his watch to point the hour of day. From an immense base formation of white silica it has built up a crater twenty feet in height, the irregular sides of which are terraced down to the level in many a fine table. These tables vary from two and a half to six feet in length, and form a succession of unique basins that receive the falling waters during an eruption. They are ever full and constantly overflowing. The jet thrown out is five by six feet in diameter, and is thrown skyward to a vertical height of one hundred and fifty feet for the space of eight to twelve minutes. Around Old Faithful will be seen a number of hot-spring formations, the description of which is hardly necessary, since so many similar ones have been before described in the Lower Basin.

Descending from Faithful directly to the river, and crossing to the other side, we first find the Beehive Geyser. This formation is modest-looking, and when not in eruption is not calculated to impress the tourist; but it is really one of the finest spouters in the basin. In shape its resembles an oldfashioned straw beehive with the apex evenly cut off. It is three feet high, five feet in diameter at the base, and has an oval orifice twenty-four by thirty-six inches. The edges of the crater are handsomely scalloped and curiously ornamented. It has no regular intervals of spouting, so far as has yet been ascertained; but the writer has seen it in eruption twice in one day. It throws a volume of water the full size of the crater to a vertical height of two hundred and nineteen feet by actual triangular measurement, and holds up its beautiful fountain for eighteen minutes at each eruption.

A little up stream, and back upon a small eminence one hundred yards from the Beehive, is the Giantess, a fine and correct illustration of which is given on another page. There is no mistaking this geyser, for its peculiarities and formation are vastly different from any other in the basin. At first one scarcely believes it to be anything more than a huge degenerating hot-spring. Its large, oval aperture is eighteen by twenty-five feet in diameter, and when not in eruption no water can be discovered. A gurgling sound, as of waters boiling furiously, comes up from below, and a constant steam-vapor is arising. The eruption, however, which occurs two or three times in twenty-four hours, is one of the grandest and most impressive spectacles ever beheld. (See "Horseback Rides.") The crater suddenly becomes filled nearly to the surface, and with a terrible spasm the whole immense body of water is projected into the air a distance of one hundred feet, and is held up to this height by successive impulses for the space of twenty minutes. Around the main aperture are six smaller ones, which send up independent jets in a circle around the main column to a height of two hundred and fifty feet, giving it the appearance of a huge fountain closely surrounded by smaller ones. The effect is sublime and fascinating. From the Giantess to the slight bend in the river below, the interval is studded with hot-spring basins of every variety, shape, and color.

The next geyser of any note on this side of the river is the Saw-Mill Geyser, perhaps one thousand yards from the Giantess, and on a direct line from Castle Geyser on the opposite bank. The Saw-Mill is a noisy and interesting geyser, but nothing to compare with its larger companions. For convenience

RIVERSIDE GEYSER.

DENTAL CUP.

sake we will keep down this side of the river, and return by the other bank.

The next after the Saw-Mill, two hundred yards distant and to the right, is Grand Geyser, a prominent rival of the Giantess. Immediately preceding its display, the surrounding surface for hundreds of yards is shaken as if by an earthquake; then suddenly a stream of water, two and a half by four feet, is shot up two hundred feet toward the clouds, while the column of steam accompanying it ascends fully one thousand feet. Nothing can excel the crystal clearness of its waters, nor none paint the majesty of its display. Within twenty feet of this orifice is another of irregular form, fifteen by twenty-five feet in diameter. The bottom of this great reservoir is covered with thick spongiform masses, and its magnificent rim is decorated with countless pearl-like beads of all sizes. Around the main reservoir are several lesser ones of most delicate shape and exquisite coloring. The Grand Geyser does not appear to be connected with the latter orifice, but the operations of one seem entirely independent of the other. The Grand Geyser has no regular time of eruption, but its displays occur at least twice in twenty-four hours.

The next that will be visited is the Riverside Geyser, several hundred yards from the Grand, and in the very water's edge of the river. Like the Saw-Mill, it is an almost constant spouter, but does not throw its jet to any great height. The crater is oddly fashioned and prettily carved. From here, keep close to the river edge for two hundred yards, and you will come upon one of the most indescribably grand geyser formations in the basin. The crater-mound is not imposing at first, but on closer examination it develops into an object of much interest. This is the Fan Geyser, and the last one of prominence on this side of the river. The entire formation is flat, and about one hundred feet in length. It has five distinct craters, and when getting ready for a display much resembles the workings of a giant stationary-engine. (See "Horseback Rides.") Its eruptions occur four or five times in twenty-four hours, each one continuing from eighteen to thirty minutes. The water from the largest crater is thrown to the vertical height of one hundred feet.

We now *cross the river* and proceed *up stream*. Bearing to the right a little over a small knoll, with one hundred and fifty yards' travel, we are standing in front of Giant Geyser, an admirable illustration of which we publish from the magic pencil of Thomas Moran the artist. While the Giantess is truly the queen, the Giant is as truly the king of wonders. Its crater-mound is fully twenty feet high, ten feet in diameter, and has an orifice four by six feet in diameter. Its formation has been likened to a broken horn or huge hollow tree that has been unevenly broken off. Its discharges are irregular, but the jet thrown out is enormous. It is thrown to a vertical height of two hundred feet, and continues uninterruptedly for *three* hours. See this monster in eruption, if possible, else you have not seen the crowning marvel of this wonderful region.

Square to the right of the Giant, close in to the timber, is the Grotto, situated on a mound of pure white silica and encircled by a cluster of hot-springs. Its unique crater-formation is its greatest feature, and to correctly describe it in words is next to impossible. Its crater rises about twenty feet, and the volume of water, four by eight feet in diameter, is thrown sixty feet upward. Eruptions occur four or five times daily. Several hundred yards farther back from the river in the same direction is the Pyramid, Punch-Bowl, Bath-Tub, and Black-Sand geysers, all of which will be easily found by keeping in a southwesterly direction from the Grotto. To describe each of them would be an unpleasant repetition of what has already been written, and we leave them to the personal inspection of the tourist.

We will now leave this group, make a detour toward the river, and up stream, five or six hundred yards to your camp among the first cluster of pines. Just beyond camp, in the direction of Old Faithful, is Castle Geyser and Circe's Boudoir. The crater and mound of Castle Geyser are very like the ruins of some ancient castle, and looms up fully forty feet above its base. The orifice is two and a half by five feet in diameter, and throws up its fountain sixty to eighty feet. No regularity is noticeable in its periods of eruption, but it has recorded four times in twenty-four hours. A full description of the Castle and Circe's Boudoir is given elsewhere.

We have now made the complete rounds of the more prominent geysers, but there are still hundreds of small geysers, hot-springs, and other marvels that are to be visited. A pleasant walk and an abundance of curiosities are afforded by crossing over to the east bank of the river at Fan Geyser, and proceeding on down stream to where Iron-Spring creek (west fork of the Fire-Hole) makes a junction with the main stream. As you cross the stream just below the fork, you will find a large group of hot-springs having a temperature of from 140° to 200°. About the centre of the group is what is called Soda Geyser, answering to the general description of the others. It is a continual spouter—ten to fifteen feet being the height of its ambition. The waters are so strongly impregnated with mineral as to make them nauseous and unfit for use. Follow along up (crossing and recrossing) Iron-Spring creek for two miles to Iron-Spring, an enormous hot-spring fairly nestled into the mountain-side. Here you can get fine specimens of wood petrifactions, crystals, etc. Directly in front of you, looking east, is the pasture alluded to. Descend to and travel directly southeast across it, striking your camp at Castle Geyser in one and a half miles. Another point of interest is the cañon across the river from Castle Geyser, *via* the Giantess to the range hemming in the basin on the east. One half mile up this gorge a splendid cluster of hot-springs and extinct geysers are located. To one not already surfeited with wonders their inspection will well repay the short journey.

On leaving the upper Geyser Basin for the Yellowstone, one is loath to take the back-track to the Lower Basin; and this is not absolutely necessary. Follow *up* the Fire-Hole river above Old Faithful; then, before getting into the marsh one mile above, cross to the east side of the river to Hayden's Trail. Keep up the east bank until the river bottom narrows to a deep cañon. The trail is forced to the top of the bank, and in the next half mile passes the beautiful cascades of the Fire-Hole. The principal fall is thirty feet high and forty feet wide. From this point the Yellowstone Trail turns directly east across a flat divide, *via* Shoshone Lake and the Shoshone Geyser Basin, to Yellowstone Lake, fifteen miles distant. If this trail is adopted, start early in the morning from the geysers, so as not to be hurried past much that is interesting. It is an eight hours' journey, with good water and grass, and brings the tourist out on the extreme western shore of the lake, and twenty miles from its foot. There is also a rough trail leading up the Fire-Hole above the Cascades to a *third* geyser basin, lying at an elevation of seventy-seven hundred feet above sea-level. This basin spreads out about three-quarters of a mile in width, and has a fine cluster of hot-springs and geysers in its northeast corner. From here on there is a difficult and indistinct trail to Madison lake, leading to other marvels. Another trail adopted by tourists is to return to lower Geyser Basin, strike to the right across the basin between the Chalk-Vat and hot lakes till you reach the timber and foot of the east-side mountains, where there is a small stream and good grazing. Here camp for the night, as it is twenty-four miles to Yellowstone river. Here again the tourist has a choice of trails—the one hereafter described coming into the Lower Basin from the Mud Volcanoes on the Yellowstone, *via* Alum Creek and Mary's Lake; and the one about to be described. On leaving camp at the timber and stream just mentioned, follow the prairie around the edge of the timber a mile or so, making a semicircle to right; pass extinct geysers; trail soon reaches a little stream and leads up it, crossing and recrossing. Trail good a few miles; then reaches a swampy prairie, and is difficult to find. On entering it, bear to the left, zigzagging in and out of the timber, keeping as close to the prairie as practicable. There are some three or four miles of this. It is the worst place on the trip, and ends the swamp business as you are travelling. Finally you strike a little brook and the trail clear and distinct. Noon here before starting up the mountain; last good water for ten miles. Get away by half-past one. The trail over the mountain is good, but steep in places for two or three miles, and reaches an altitude of seventy-nine hundred feet. Lakes, old craters, and brimstone-vents on top of range. Splendid trail down the mountain; comes out on nice brook full of fish. As you get out in open flat country the trail becomes indistinct; *keep general direction if you lose trail,* and you will strike the river near a clump of timber at the Mud Volcano. Turn up river, pass volcano, and camp in timber next the river a hundred yards above volcano.

To the Yellowstone lake, from this point, is six miles. It is a splendid trail and a glorious morning ride; plenty of feathered game. You are now at the foot of Yellowstone lake, without doubt the most wonderful and beautiful body of water in the world. Dr. Hayden, United States Geologist, and Mr. Jas.

Stevenson, his able assistant, have made this curious lake a thorough study, and to them the author is principally indebted for the data concerning it. Here at an altitude of seventy-four hundred and twenty-seven feet, surrounded by bold mountain-peaks, lifting up their snow-covered crests eleven thousand feet above the sea, you have a body of water thirty miles in length, fifteen miles in breadth from west to east, with soundings of from one and a half to fifty fathoms, a body of water sufficient to float the navies of the world! Its shore-line or circumference measures over three hundred miles. Some idea may be had of its great altitude, which the tourist does not at first realize, by considering the fact that if Mount Washington, the pride of New England, should be placed at the foot of the lake, with its base at sea-level, the sparkling waters of this mountain sea *would roll two thousand feet above its summit!* There is only need here of a brief description, as the tourist will explore and admire it in person. Our illustration gives but a faint conception of its beauty or surroundings. The shore on the east side for five miles is a broad and level beach of sand, and the lake is shallow for some distance out. This sand is composed almost entirely of obsidian and those minute and beautiful crystals known as California diamonds; and with the sun shining brightly, it sparkles and flashes as if it were indeed composed of a bed of cut diamonds, rubies, and emeralds. The name of Diamond Beach has been most appropriately given to this section of the shore, but to whom we are indebted for the name is unknown to the author.

Continuing on up the shore beyond Pelican (the first) creek, putting in from that side, numerous hot-springs are found. Indeed, there is a chain of hot-springs and mud-caldrons encircling the entire lake. These springs are even more wonderful and beautiful than those of Fire-Hole Basin. The funnel-

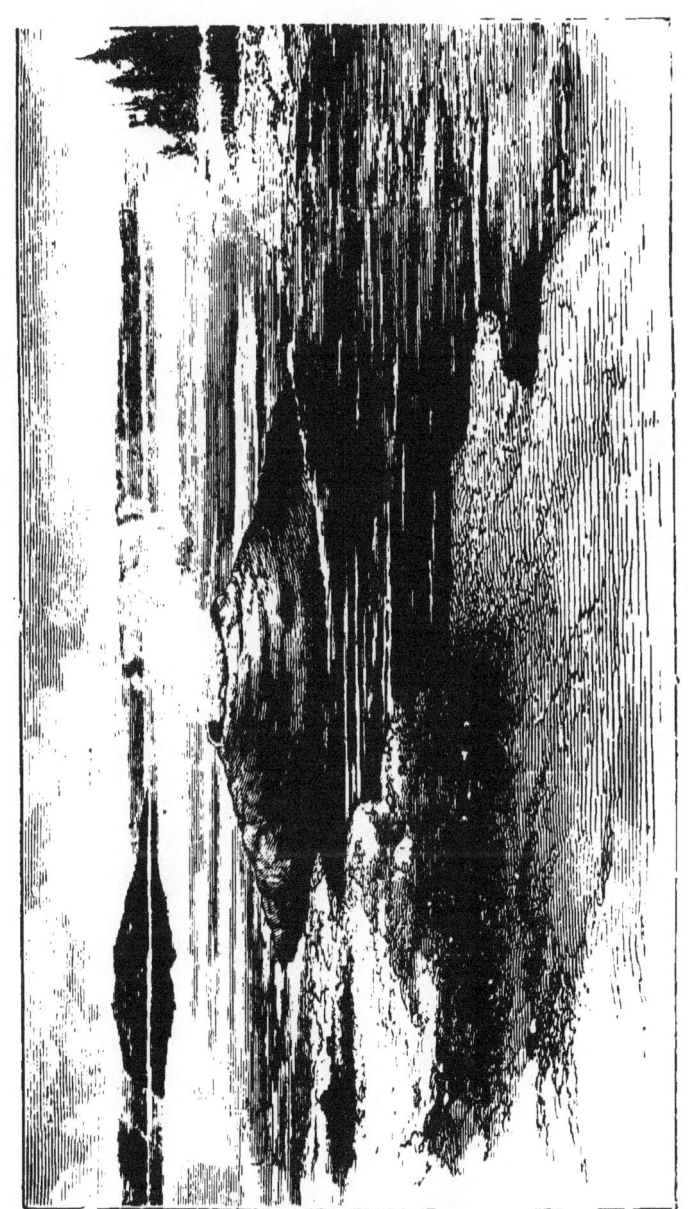

HOT-SPRING CONE.

shaped craters of some (see illustration) extend so far out into the lake that one can stand upon the silicious mound, catch salmon-trout, and without changing position, drop them into the hot water of the spring and cook them *without removing them from the line.* This statement seems incredible, but is nevertheless a fact, as Sir William Blackmore, a distinguished Englishman who visited the lake in 1872, easily accomplished the feat. To follow the shore-line of the lake the entire distance around is a tedious task, as there are many marshes to cross and much brushwood and fallen timber to be encountered. Yet to the sportsman the trip is full of interest and adventure, as the region abounds in elk, deer, moose, cinnamon, black, and grizzly bear, catamounts, and mountain-lion. Be careful they do not hunt *you,* instead of you hunting *them.* The better course for the tourist is to select a permanent camp while at the lake, and from it explore the surrounding forests, and with boats visit its beautiful islands. The most prominent of these lies near the lower end, and is named Stevenson's Island, after the gallant young explorer who has accompanied and so efficiently assisted Dr. Hayden in his numerous surveys. Directly east from this is Steamboat Point and Pelican Roost, and above and about the centre of the lake is Frank's Island; a mile to the northwest is Dot Island. A week can be profitably spent in this manner.

After leaving the lake, the tourist will retrace his steps down the west bank of Yellowstone river, over a plain trail, *via* Mud Volcano, Cascade creek, Upper and Lower falls, and Grand Cañon of the Yellowstone, Tower creek and falls, Mammoth Hot-Springs on Gardner's river, the Devil's Slide on the Yellowstone, Botteller's Ranch, Trail creek, Spring creek, and Fort Ellis, to Bozeman—all of which are described in the route from Bozeman.

THE ROUTE FROM BOZEMAN.

The tourist starting from Bozeman to make the Grand Rounds of the Park, will go over an excellent wagon-road, seventy-five miles in length, *via* Fort Ellis, (three miles,) a short visit to and inspection of which will interest those who have never visited the far west military posts of the United States. Fort Ellis is the most important military post in the territory, protecting as it does the settlements on the Yellowstone and Gallatin valleys from the incursions of hostile Indians.

Four miles beyond you enter a rocky cañon through which runs a branch of the East Gallatin river. This cañon is seven miles in length, and is one of much beauty. The walls are composed of limestone, and by the action of the elements have been worn and carved into a thousand fantastic shapes. Following up this stream you reach a small divide in the hill. This leads out to the head of Trail creek, twelve miles from Bozeman; you follow Trail creek down twelve miles and to within five miles of the Yellowstone, when it would be well to camp for dinner, if you have taken an early morning start from Bozeman. The first view of Yellowstone river and valley is picturesque and grand, covering a vista of some thirty miles along the valley and river, which is here several miles wide and shut in by volcanic mountains of immense height on the opposite side. Heavy masses of snow fill the upper ravines and gorges in the summer-time—feeders of hundreds of springs which trickle valleyward through dense evergreen forests on the mountain sides. The valley descends from the foot-hills in gentle declivities covered with luxuriant grass, and numberless streams course down the mountain ranges on either side. Almost in front of you, on the opposite side of the Yellowstone, is Emigrant's Peak, ten thousand three hundred and ninety feet above sea-level;

DIKE AND COLUMNS OF BRECCIA.

and several miles away to the right, Pyramid Mountain. Descending to and following up the Yellowstone valley over the Bozeman and National Park carriage-way, the next point will be Botteler's Ranch, thirty-nine miles from Bozeman. Here will be found a fine camping-place or accommodation at Botteler's Hotel, as tourists may decide. Leaving Botteler's, the road follows up the river, crossing two mountain tributaries, and six miles above passes over Point of Rocks. Four miles farther on it enters the Second cañon of the Yellowstone. The road here is fairly hewn from the rocks above the stream. Passing through and ten miles above the cañon, to the right is Cinnabar Mountain. A portion of this mountain, from its rugged character and peculiar formation, is called the Devil's Slide. On either side of "the slide," which is one hundred and fifty feet wide, covered with grass, and traces the mountain from summit to base, rises a perpendicular wall of yellowish gray quartz fifty feet thick and two hundred feet high, the whole forming a marvellous feature of nature's handiwork. From Cinnabar Mountain to the mouth of Gardner's river and the Third cañon is six miles.

Here you leave the Yellowstone river and follow up Gardner's river four miles to White Mountain Hot-springs, the end of the wagon-road, and seventy-five miles from Bozeman. Here will be found fair hotel accommodation, supplies, guides, pack and saddle animals, to supply deficiencies.

This group of springs is pronounced by all, the most wonderful of any in the National Park—not that the springs differ materially from those of the Geyser Basins, but because of the immense and curious formations which their centuries of overflow has builded. The calcareous deposits of these springs cover an area of about two miles square, and the active springs extend from the margin of the river, five thousand five hundred and forty-five feet, to an elevation nearly one thousand feet above, or six thousand five hundred and twenty-two feet above sea-level. It is almost vain to attempt a description of this marvellous deposit. It comprises so many separate wonders, and is in itself so massive, curious, and grand, that the eye alone can convey an adequate conception to the mind. The steep sides of the mountain are ornamented with a series of semi-circular basins or reservoirs, with margins varying in height from a few inches to six and eight feet, and so beautifully scolloped and adorned with snowy bead-work, that the beholder is amazed. Add to this a snow-white ground of silica, with every variety and shade of scarlet, green, and yellow, as brilliant as the brightest of analine dyes. These reservoirs are of all sizes, shapes, and peculiarities, and extend from the summit to the base of the mountain. At the very top of the mountain there is a broad, flat terrace of two hundred yards area. Near its margin is the largest and most active hot-spring in the group. It is twenty-five by forty feet in diameter, and so transparent is the boiling pool, that one can look down into the beautiful ultramarine depth to the very bottom of the basin. The sides of this great hot-water reservoir are ornamented with coral-like forms, with every variety of coloring, from pure white to bright cream-yellow, and the blue sky reflected in the transparent waters gives an azure-tint to the whole which far surpasses all art. The author does not deem it necessary to dwell longer on the beauty and curiosities which cluster everywhere around this huge structure of nature's architecture, as he has given it prominent notice elsewhere in this volume. The noted points are the Liberty Cap, fifty feet high and twenty feet diameter at the base, standing on the first terrace of the mountain; Dead Chimney, Bath Pools, and Grotto in the Glen—all of which are easily found and attractive.

Leaving White Mountain Hot-springs, the horseback trail crosses and leads along the margin of Gardner's river, and up a steep hill out of the cañon. Going up this ascent and looking up the stream, the tourist is afforded a fine view of Gardner River Falls. The stream pours over a declivity of three hundred feet, forming a beautiful and romantic cascade. The direct fall is one hundred feet. The constant roar of the rushing waters is pleasant to the ear, and the almost hidden cataract greatly tempts an inspection.

Eighteen miles farther on are Tower Falls and Cañon. Tower falls is one of the most picturesque in the whole region. The stream passes down through a dark and rocky cañon hundreds of feet in depth, and two hundred yards from where it empties into the Yellowstone, is precipitated in one unbroken sheet a sheer descent of one hundred and fifty-six feet, into a rocky gorge below. At the top of the fall, and surrounding it on every side, are tall spires of rock, fifty to one hundred feet high—some of them standing upon the very brink of the precipice, like giant sentinels for ever guarding the fairy waters. The sides of the chasm are worn away into gloomy caverns, lined with variously-tinted mosses, nourished by the spray of the cataract. Nothing can be more chastely beautiful than this lovely cascade, hidden away in the dim light of overshadowing rocks and pines—its very voice a low murmur, and almost unheard at a distance of five hundred yards. A fine view can be had from the cliff above them, and a better one by walking down to the mouth of Tower creek, two hundred yards, and following up stream to the sheet. Two hundred yards above the falls, below where the trail crosses the creek, is a finely-sheltered camp, grass, wood, and water.

Leaving Tower falls the trail veers to the west of the Yellowstone, and crosses the basin about one mile west of Mount Washburn. This mountain is the highest peak in this portion of the range—nine thousand nine hundred and ninety-six feet above sea-level, and from its summit can be obtained a birdseye view of the National Park. You can ride to the summit in an hour, and then have a clear, unobstructed view of over one hundred miles in every direction. To the southeast is the great basin of Yellowstone lake, spreading out in a vast panorama of water, shore, and tree, for many miles; beyond it, still to the south, the Three Tetons are rising high above their fellows, with their cloud-piercing summits covered with perpetual snow, the monarchs of all they survey. To the southwest a dense pine forest extends for one hundred miles, without a single peak rising above the black, level mass; a little farther to the southwest and west are the Madison mountains, a lofty, grand, snow-capped range, extending far to the northward; nearer and in full view to the west, commence the bold peaks of the Gallatin range, which extends north as far as the eye can reach; to the north is a full view of the valley of the Yellowstone, and the imposing range that walls it in. Emigrant Peak, and the splendid group of mountains of which it forms so prominent a part, can be clearly seen, and lose none of their marvellous beauty of outline, view them from what point you may. Farther to the east and north are the Big Horn mountains. The whole scene is sublime and well repays the ascent. From Mount Washburn to the Lower falls and Grand Cañon of the Yellowstone, is a distance of eighteen miles, over a fair trail, with enough hill-climbing to give good appetites for supper. The trail runs along the side of the mountain, then descends into a cañon and again ascends very abruptly to the crest which divides the rest of the world from Yellowstone Basin. All along this portion of the route many beautiful and curious wild flowers may be seen and gathered. At the foot of Mount Washburn, on its southeastern side, is a wonderful group of mud-springs, called

Hell Broth Springs. They are worth visiting, and if the tourist desires to make the detour, he must camp one and a half miles from the top of the range just ascended, on a small stream where there is everything to make camp pleasant. Follow this creek down for one mile and the springs will be found. This is about five miles, with plain trail, from the Lower falls. Arriving at the falls, the tourist will find several good camping-places—one in a little wood-encircled depression back from the cañon, two hundred yards. If you camp here, to get good drinking-water you must carry it from Cascade creek, a few hundred yards away, although there is plenty of water for the horses close by, in some "coolies." The falls are so thoroughly described in the Horseback Rides, that the author will here only give the main features. The waters of Yellowstone river at this point make a clear leap of three hundred and ninety feet to the bottom of the cañon below, and as a spectacle of grandeur and sublimity, Yellowstone falls are surpassed by none in the universe. There are many points from which good views may be obtained, but those we consider the finest are from the brink of the precipice, and from a point in the cañon wall one-fourth of a mile below. With a little patience and labor the descent to the top of the sheet may be made. From this point the grandest view of the cañon is had. No language can do justice to a description of this marvel of grandeur, and our illustration gives but a limited idea of the real. The very nearly vertical walls have a slight slope down to the water's edge on either side, so that from the summit the river appears like a thread of silver tracing the rocky bottom; the variegated colors of the sides—yellow, red, brown, white—all intermixed and shading into each other; the gothic columns of every form standing out from the walls, put Art to blush and Nature in smiles. The margins of the cañon on either side are fringed with evergreens, and the whole scene is clothed with a splendor that speaks of Divinity. The walls vary in height from two thousand to two thousand five hundred feet.

The Upper falls are one-fourth of a mile above the Lower ones, and by some are pronounced even more beautiful than their proud rival. The Yellowstone here, after having rushed over two beautiful cascades of thirty and forty feet, respectively, plunge over a perpendicular cliff of one hundred and forty feet vertical height. The sheet as it goes over is one hundred feet wide, and the entire volume is detached into the most beautiful shower of snow-white beads. As the stream strikes the rocky basin below, it shoots through the water with a ricochet for two hundred feet. Above the falls the Upper river is calm and placid, and looking at it one would scarcely believe it was about to take these two wild leaps to the lower world. Between the Upper and Lower falls the tourist will cross Cascade creek, so called from a handsome cascade formed by the stream in tumbling pell-mell over a series of rocky ledges. Cascade creek flows here at an altitude of seventy-seven hundred and eighty-seven feet above the sea, and below the divide of the mountain one thousand feet.

Leaving the vicinity of the falls the tourist will take the trail leading along the river, until it opens out into a level prairie country three miles to the left of Sulphur mountain. There being no good camping-place at Sulphur mountain, you will go on three miles farther to the Mud volcano, nine miles from Cascade creek, where a good camp can be selected. From this point to Yellowstone lake is a distance of ten miles, over a good trail, keeping close to the river the entire distance. Here at the Mud volcano, the trail of the Bozeman route and that of the Virginia route, form a junction, (see Virginia route for trip to and around Yellowstone lake,) and from this point the tourist coming from Bozeman and desiring to visit the Geyser Basins, is afforded two routes. One is that described in the Virginia route, and the other is called the Alum creek and Mary's lake route. There is scarcely any difference in the distance over the two, and either is very attractive. Following the Alum creek and Mary's lake trail, strike due northwest to Factory Springs on Alum creek, passing a group of three lone pines about midway of the plateau. These springs are five miles nearly west from Sulphur mountain. They abound in interest, and the formations are very beautiful. A good place for nooning. From here the trail is plain, good and well-watered, all the way to Lower Geyser Basin, nineteen miles. It first passes over a small mountain to the right, and crosses Alum creek. From the top of this mountain the plateau extends to the summit of the range, with sulphur and other springs on the way. Coming up the mountain, on the very summit of the range dividing the waters of the Yellowstone and Madison rivers, the trail passes to one side of Mary's lake, one of those beautiful wonders so peculiar to the National Park region. This lake is one-and-a-half miles in circumference. It is completely encircled by tall pines and firs, and when its quiet surface is struck by the sun's rays shimmering through the dense foliage, it has the reflecting powers of a huge mirror of plate-glass. Sky, tree, and spectator, are miraged in its clear depths, and it seems a miniature fairy-sea into which the mountain snow-streams find a rest from their wanderings. The name is already claimed for several ladies of note, but if you have a sister or sweetheart bearing the title of "Mary," you are at perfect liberty to rechristen it.

Leaving Mary's lake, the descent of the mountain for the next half mile is very steep, but even ladies can keep the saddle without danger. After the descent is made, the trail leads across an open country due west, to and down a branch of the Madison river; crosses the stream several times, but runs near it until within a few miles of the Lower Basin. The ride from the Mud volcano or Sulphur mountain to the Lower Geyser Basin, is a pleasant one day's ride. Arriving at the basin, the tourist again strikes the Virginia route, and, of course, follows it through as before described, to the "Wonders," and in and between both Geyser Basins, and out via the upper Fire-Hole river and Shoshone Geyser and lake to Yellowstone lake, and thence down the Yellowstone river; or, returning to the Lower Basin, go down the Madison river *via* Henry's lake to Virginia; or, over the trail to Mud volcano, and thence Bozemanward.

The author has been unable, in this first edition of The Guide, to publish a map of the trails described, but shall add this feature in the next year's edition. A very accurate map of the Park is given, however, with the aid of which, and the description of the different trails, the tourist cannot get bewildered.

WHERE AND HOW TO OUTFIT FOR THE TRIP.

Tourists can either buy or hire pack and saddle animals at Virginia or Bozeman, or can go in wagons to the Geyser Basins from Virginia, or to White Mountain Hot-springs from Bozeman. A supply of horses, equipments, etc., can be had at either place, to complete the journey on horseback. Tourists should supply themselves with a suit of warm, substantial clothing, stout boots, broad-rimmed hat, as protection from the sun. Ladies should select warm and stout garments, rather than stylish ones; coarse shoes, mosquito-nets, if early in the season, and other creature-comforts that good taste will suggest. One pack-animal is sufficient for two persons, if they do not carry too many delicacies. The entire expense of making the grand rounds from Virginia or Bozeman, will not exceed $50 to each person, with ordinary economy. A sufficient supply of shot-guns, rifles, and fishing-tackle, should accompany each party, as game and fish are abundant throughout. Light canvas-boats will come in play on Yellowstone lake and in the Madison Basin, while exploring the islands or gunning for water-fowl. If you have a good spaniel or retriever, he will be useful to bring in game, and a pack of deer or blood-hounds will furnish the sportsman fine amusement among the bear, deer, and elk.

In the back portion of this book will be found a list of business-houses. Trade with the men who advertise. Virginia and Bozeman each have ample and good hotel accommodation at fair prices, say $3 to $4 per day. Saddle-horses may be had for from $60 to $125 each. The merchants will supply all necessaries, and the conveniences of each town are complete and extensive.

A BRIEF GENERAL DESCRIPTION

OF

MONTANA TERRITORY;

ITS VALLEYS, RIVERS, CITIES, AND TOWNS.

The author feels no need of making an apology for including in this work the following brief general description of Montana Territory, as this delightful Rocky Mountain portion of the United States, with its wonderful treasure-houses of native gold, silver, and the baser metals, its gorgeous mountain scenery, its fertile and verdure-clad valleys, crystal rivers, and beautiful inland lakes, and its health-giving climate, is fast attracting the attention of not alone the older settled states, but even that of Europe herself. What could there then be more appropriately published, in connection with the wonders of the National Park, than a description of the region which holds the only key of entrance to this mountain-locked museum of marvels? The tourist to the Park will pass through it and admire it; hunt the elk, buffalo, moose, bear, deer, and antelope which graze and roam over its mountains, plains, and valleys; and will delight to fish in its thousands of trout streams for the speckled trophies that are in every land the angler's pride. It will then only be natural that he should desire to know more of the country than can be seen in the chase or through the field-glass. The ambitious, adventurous young man of the Eastern and Western states and cities will scan its history with interest, and can here find a worthy field for his ambition and energy—a practical knowledge of that, to most young men of the East only dreamed of, the territory known as the Rocky Mountains.

It is the intention of the writer to avoid verbosity and tediousness, and to convey a correct idea of the formation and resources of the territory in the fewest number of pages possible. To this end he has drawn somewhat upon the information furnished to government through scientific reports, and to it added what information a long residence in the mountains has afforded him.

Montana, with the exception of Alaska, is the most recently organized territory of the United States. Embracing that region lying between the forty-fifth and forty-ninth parallels of north latitude, and one hundred and fourth and one hundred and sixteenth meridians of west longitude, it contains an area of 143,776 square miles or 92,016,640 acres, extending from east to west about five hundred and fifty miles, and from north to south about two hundred and eighty miles. It is separated into two very unequal areas by the dividing range of the Rocky Mountains, which forms the southwestern boundary from the west line of Wyoming to the intersection of 45° 40' north latitude and the one hundred and fourteenth meridian. Here it suddenly bends eastward for some distance, and then runs north about twenty degrees west to the northern boundary of the territory. About one-fifth of the entire area belongs to the Pacific slope, being drained by the head-waters of the Columbia, and four-fifths to the Atlantic slope, being drained by the Missouri and its tributaries. Extending from the mouth of the Yellowstone to the summit of Bitter-Root range, about two-fifths belong to the mountain region, three-fifths consisting of broad open plains lying east of the Rocky Mountain range. The mountain belt, which forms a broad margin along the western end, has probably an average width (direct measurement from the summit of the Bitter-Root range to the east flank of the Rocky Mountains) of one hundred and seventy-five miles, running northwest parallel to the western boundary. Besides these two leading ranges and their interlocking spurs on the western slope, there are some minor ranges on the eastern side, which though comparatively small in extent, are important in respect to the influence they have upon the course of the water-drainage and the form and direction of the principal valleys. In the northwest corner of Wyoming, near the point where the dividing range makes the western bend and passes out of this territory, is what appears to be the great mountain nucleus of this region. Here the Big Horn, Yellowstone, Madison, Snake, and Green rivers have their origin. From this mountain centre a number of short ranges run northward, giving direction to a number of streams, and appearing like evidences of the abortive efforts of the elevating force to keep up its direct course. Along the southern border the Snow mountains—the northern extension of the Big Horn range—penetrate for a short distance into the territory, compelling the Yellowstone to make a grand detour in order to sweep around the northern flank. In the central portion are the Belt, Judith, and Highwood mountains, forming an irregular group of short and broken ranges, around which the Missouri sweeps to the northward before entering upon its long eastward stretch. These also have a central nucleus situated in the western part of Meagher county, where the Musselshell, Judith, Deep, and Shields rivers take their rise. North of the Missouri river the plain is interrupted only by Bear's Paw, the Little Rockies, and occasional Tetons.

The elevations of both mountains and valleys, as

will be seen from the list of elevations presented below, is much less than that of the great mountain belt of Colorado and Wyoming, and even that of New Mexico, Utah, and Nevada.

ELEVATIONS ABOVE THE SEA LEVEL.

	Feet.
Fort Union, mouth of the Yellowstone	2,022
Fort Benton, Missouri river	2,780
Forks of Sun river	4,114
Lewis and Clark Pass	6,519
Blackfoot Fork, near mouth of Salmon-trout creek	3,966
Missoula river, near junction of St. Regis de Borgia	2,897
Summit of Cœur d'Alene mountains, near the Pass	5,089
Fort Owen, Bitter-Root Valley	3,284
Deer Lodge City, Deer Lodge Valley	4,768
Prickly Pear Valley, near Helena	4,000
Mullen's Pass	6,283

From this list we see that the western basin reaches a depression less than three thousand feet above the sea level, and that the least altitudes of the Eastern Slopes range from two thousand and twenty-two to four thousand feet above the sea level.

The entire territory may be divided into four sections, each having its water system and natural boundaries tolerably well defined, as follows: The northwestern, which includes all that portion lying between the Rocky Mountain and the Bitter-Root Range; the southern, which is drained by the three forks of the Missouri; the southeastern, which is drained by the Yellowstone; and the northern, which includes the valleys of Milk and Missouri rivers, and the bordering plains.

THE NORTHWESTERN SECTION. This section, as before stated, is situated between the Rocky Mountain range on the east and the Bitter-Root and Cœur d'Alene mountains on the west, extending from the forty-sixth parallel of latitude to the British Possessions, and including all of Missoula county and the southern half of Deer Lodge county. It is about one hundred and fifty miles wide and two hundred miles long, containing an area of thirty thousand square miles; and is traversed from southeast to northwest by Clark's Fork of the Columbia and its leading tributaries.

The northern part is variable in character, having some open prairie country and valleys of limited extent, while much of it is broken and rugged, and covered with heavy pine forests. It is drained by Flathead river, which has three leading tributaries: Maple river, coming from the northwest; Flathead, from the north; and another branch from the northeast. Near the forty-eighth parallel this stream expands into a beautiful lake about thirty miles long and ten or twelve miles wide. Below this it is of considerable size, flows in a southwest direction for about fifty miles, and joins the Missoula, the two forming Clark's Fork.*

On the west side, near its southern limit, starts a range of broken and somewhat rugged hills, which extends northwest to the vicinity of Kootenay river, in the extreme northwest angle of the territory. This range, which forms a divide between the waters of Maple river and those of Clark's Fork, is mostly covered with dense pine forests. The country, in the vicinity of Kootenay river, is composed chiefly of high rolling prairies, through which this stream, here some two or three hundred yards in width, flows with a moderate current. The immediate valley of this river is from five to fifteen miles wide, and well grassed, affording excellent range for cattle, horses, and sheep to an almost unlimited number. The soil is fairly susceptible of profitable cultivation, as is evidenced by the experiments, in a small way, made

* The main branch of this stream has a number of different names. From the junction of Deer Lodge and Little Blackfoot rivers to the mouth of Big Blackfoot, it is called Hell-Gate river; from there to the mouth of the Flathead it is called Missoula; from there it retains the original name of Clark's Fork, though it is sometimes called Columbia.

by the Kootenay Indians, who have tilled portions of it for years.

For twenty miles Tobacco creek, a tributary of the Kootenay, runs through an open prairie country. It rises in the forest-clad range before mentioned, and runs northwest. Maple river, for most of its course, to its junction with the Flathead, traverses a forest-covered section, its valley being narrow, until it enters the prairie. North of the lake there is a prairie some thirty miles in length, north and south, and fifteen to twenty miles wide, one arm of which extends northwest, in the direction of Maple river, and the other north.

On the east side of the lake (Flathead) the country is broken and mountainous, and heavily timbered with pine and fir; the western side also has fine timber, but not in so large quantity. Below the lake, Flathead river is from one hundred to one hundred and fifty yards wide, and from two to three feet deep, with occasionally small rapids and falls. Hot-Spring creek, which rises some distance west of the lake, flows southeast about twenty-five miles, and enters Flathead river opposite the Pen d'Orville Mission. In the vicinity of this stream, and particularly along its shores, there is a large area of rich farming lands, as yet wholly untouched by pre-emptions. The valleys of the Flathead, and the little streams flowing into it from the east, also afford another large area of valuable farming lands, which will not long remain unoccupied by the settler.

Jocko river runs through one of the prettiest valleys in this entire section. It is in the form of a triangle, its sides, which are nearly equal, being from ten to twelve miles long. It contains about fifty square miles, most of which can be easily irrigated, and which, if properly cultivated, will produce bountiful crops, the soil being quite fertile. Surrounded by lofty mountains, which form its triangular walls, little rills flow down into it from all sides, furnishing a never-failing supply of pure, clear water. In 1870 the Indian agent, with but little help except that of the squaws, (the Indian men being generally too lazy to work,) raised over one thousand bushels of potatoes, fifteen hundred bushels of wheat, three hundred bushels of corn, etc.; his corn, as he reports, yielding as much as seventy-five bushels to the acre.

This portion of the section has but few settlements in it, Jocko Valley being the principal one; north of the lake but little is known in regard to it, but upon many of the little streams which flow down from the mountains will be found small arable areas amply supplied with water for irrigation. And here, as well as on the western side of the section, many of these minor valleys are covered with forests of pine, fir, and other varieties of coniferous trees.

The southern district, which is somewhat quadrilateral, is surrounded on three sides by leading mountain ranges, the Rocky Mountain divide forming its southern and eastern boundary, and the Bitter-Root mountain its west. It has three principal streams, which converge toward the northwest angle, where they unite to form the Missoula river, as follows: the Hell-Gate, (the continuation of Deer Lodge,) rising in the southeast angle, runs northwest diagonally through the district; the Bitter-Root, rising in the southwest angle, runs north near the western border; and the Big Blackfoot, rising in the Rocky Mountains to the east, runs westward along the northern border. All that portion lying south of Hell-Gate river is traversed north and south by a series of somewhat parallel ridges, separated by intervening valleys of greater or less width, each drained by one leading stream. The most important of these valleys, in an agricultural point of view, are those watered by the Deer Lodge and Bitter-Root rivers. Deer Lodge valley is about forty miles long, with an average width of twelve miles of good farming lands. The grazing is without limit. The soil of this valley is good, being covered in a natural state with a heavy growth of rich and nutritious grasses, and now yields abundant crops of wheat, oats, rye, barley, and vegetables to the thrifty people who have there settled. Not only is it supplied with abundant water by the central stream which traverses the entire length of the valley, but there are quite a number of smaller rivulets coming in from either side. The elevation above the sea is nearly five thousand feet at Deer Lodge City. Mr. Granville Stuart, a gentleman who has kept a careful meteorological record for the past twelve years, the observations being taken at Deer Lodge City, tells us the yearly mean temperature will not vary materially from 40.7, and the mean of the seasons as follows: spring, 41.6; summer, 69.7; autumn, 43.1; winter, 19.9. It must be remembered that this record, which shows a somewhat rigorous climate, was made at an altitude of forty-seven hundred and sixty-eight feet above the level of the sea, and is consequently far below the mean temperature of the principal agricultural areas of the territory; and in addition to this, the peculiar open position of Deer Lodge City renders it more exposed to winter storms than other portions of the same section. The total yearly rain-fall is set down as being from sixteen to seventeen inches, and for the growing season, (April to July,) 9.15 inches.

The valley is pretty well settled along its lower half. Deer Lodge City, one of the principal, and probably the prettiest town of the territory, is here.

Little Blackfoot, coming down from the dividing range, and having to wind its way through a mass of heavy hills, is hemmed in closely for most of its length, and affords but a narrow strip of arable land; but wherever a level space is found the soil is rich and productive, and covered with a green carpet of tall, rich grass. This valley, for part of its length, affords a roadway for travel and stage line from Helena, by way of Mullen's Pass, to Deer Lodge and points west. The bordering hills are generally well timbered.

Moving west from Deer Lodge river, there is, as has already been stated, a succession of ridges and valleys running north and south parallel to each other. Of the latter, Flint Creek Valley is the first we reach. It is divided into two parts, an upper and a lower, by a gorge some four or five miles long. The upper portion is about ten miles long, with an average width of four or five miles, including that part of the bordering hills which can be irrigated. The lower part is about fifteen miles long, and, counting the valleys of both forks, has an average width of about five miles. The climate here is rather milder than that of Deer Lodge. The grazing is good. It is but sparsely settled.

Passing westward across another ridge, we enter the narrow and rough valley of Stone creek. This stream is of considerable length, and is about the size of Deer Lodge river, (sixty to seventy-five feet wide,) very rapid and rough, flowing over boulders and ledges. Very little farming land is to be found along its banks, but the stream will furnish excellent water power, and timber is abundant along the bordering hills.

The next and last valley toward the west is that of Bitter-Root river, which contains some of the finest agricultural lands in the territory. From the mouth of the cañon, where the stream emerges from the mountains, it stretches directly north to Hell-Gate river, a distance of eighty miles. From Fort Owen, south, it varies in width from five to fifteen miles, averaging nine or ten miles. It is all well adapted to agriculture, the soil being a rich dark loam, mixed with sand and gravel. In watering its valley, the central stream, which is here of considerable size, is aided by a number of small creeks which flow into it mostly from the ridge to the east, of which the following may be enumerated in the order they come, beginning at the head of the valley: Weeping Child, Skarkahoe, Gird, Willow, Burnt Fork, Three-Mile, Six-Mile and Bouges creek, all entering from the east; and Nez Perces and Lo-Lo Forks from the west. This valley has a rich agricultural area of over four hundred thousand acres. The mean temperature is 47°, but the best means of judging of its climate is a list of its productions, so far as experiments have been attempted.

Not only can wheat, oats, barley, rye, and the hardier vegetables be raised, but Indian corn, of a tolerably good quality, is grown here year after year in sufficient quantity to supply the wants of the valley; melons, tobacco, and broom-corn thrive; and such fruits as apples, pears, plums, and cherries are matured here. Peach-trees have been planted, and it is quite probable that after a few years' trial and the trees become somewhat acclimated, they will succeed. Muskmelons, squashes, tomatoes, beets, carrots, and onions, of excellent quality and of large size, are also raised in abundance. These facts give undoubted evidence of the comparative mildness of the climate in this northern latitude.

The following sketch by Major Wheeler, the United States marshal of the territory, who passed through this and the adjacent valleys in the early part of the autumn of 1870, will convey a better idea of the beauty and agricultural resources of this part of the section than a more lengthened description. Speaking of the farm of Hon. W. E. Bass, he says:

"The large fields of wheat, oats, corn, barley, rye, and potatoes, the vegetable-garden, and especially the flower-garden, excited our admiration. We saw fifty acres of wheat, averaging forty bushels to the acre, and twenty acres of corn, averaging fifty bushels, ripe and sound. Everything else was in the same ratio. I brought away specimens of corn, onions, melons, tobacco, broom-corn, and even peanuts, which for quality and size cannot be surpassed anywhere. The flower-garden was a gem of its kind, covering half an acre, and containing over a hundred varieties. The barn is one hundred and sixty-five feet long and sixty wide. The loft will hold one hundred and fifty tons of hay, and the stalls below will accommodate the herd of dairy-cows, fifty of which are milked and the butter churned by water-power obtained from a small stream which irrigates the garden," a very convenient contrivance, becoming quite common in this territory. "The house is prettily located among shady pine-trees, a forest of which extends back to the mountains. A saw-mill furnishes the lumber used on the place. On the opposite side of the valley, ten miles away, is the farm of Thomas Harris, Esq. He has seventy acres of wheat, fifty of which are raised without irrigation, and the whole will average about forty bushels to the acre; twenty acres being a voluntary crop. Mr. Harris has an orchard of apple and plum trees of four years' growth, and they look very thrifty, varying from six to nine feet in height. Frost has never injured a twig. He has a field of timothy-grass, from which he cut twenty tons of excellent hay, or two tons to the acre. Here were vegetables of the best quality in the greatest profusion—watermelons, muskmelons, squashes, tomatoes, beets, carrots, and onions, of large growth."

The banks of the streams are lined with cotton-wood and pine, the former reaching a height of seventy to eighty feet, and the latter sometimes one hundred and fifty feet high and of three feet diameter. Although there is considerable timber between Deer Lodge and Bitter-Root valleys, yet it may be considered an open country, furnishing a large number of extensive grazing fields. In fact, it may truly be said that all of Montana, from the east flank of the Belt Mountains to the Bitter-Root Range, is one vast pasture.

It will be seen from the foregoing description of this Northwestern Section that it contains a large number of arable areas, and an ample supply of never-failing streams; while the vast amount of grazing lands and immense districts of pine forests puts the aggregate natural wealth of the section beyond definite calculation.

SOUTHERN SECTION. This section includes that portion of the territory drained by the three forks of the Missouri, viz., the Jefferson, Madison, and Gallatin rivers, and the regions as far north as Helena. It is bounded on the south, west, and partly on the north, by the Rocky Mountain Range, on the east by the divide, which separates the waters of the Gallatin from those of the Yellowstone, and embraces Beaver-Head, Jefferson, Madison, and part of Gallatin counties. It is so irregular in form that it is difficult to estimate its area, but this probably amounts to fifteen thousand square miles.

The physical geography of this section, and especially the mountain regions surrounding it, is very interesting, as here some of the great rivers of the West have their origin. Here the great Missouri, which traverses an area of sufficient size for an empire, originates. In the mountain area, in the extreme northwestern corner of Wyoming Territory, which borders on this section, the Big-Horn, Yellowstone, Madison, Green, and Snake rivers all take their rise, the first three finding an outlet for their waters through the Mississippi to the Gulf of Mexico; the next through the Colorado to the Gulf of California; and the last through the Columbia to the Pacific ocean, three thousand miles from the exit of the first. Here, amid a collection of the most wonderful scenery of the continent, is found the chief radiating point of the water systems of the Northwest. A minor radiating centre is also found in the western part of Meagher county, where the Musselshell, Judith, Deep, and Shield's rivers, all take their rise within a small area.

Mr. Stuart divides what is here given as one section into two basins, the one drained by Jefferson river and its tributaries, the other being drained by the North and South Bowlder creeks and a few small tributaries of the Missouri below the junction of the three forks. The first basin embraces all of Beaver-

Head county and the western half of Madison, and is drained by three streams, the Big-Hole (or Wisdom) river, Beaver-Head, and Stinking Water, which unite at the northeast angle to form the Jefferson. The first of these rising in the extreme western part of the section, following the course of the great bend of the range, sweeps round in a semicircle, and bursting through an intervening ridge, unites with the Beaver-Head immediately south of Deer Lodge Pass. Its valley is crescent-shaped, and not far from eighty miles in length and from ten to twenty miles in width. Big-Hole Prairie, which forms a part of this valley, is about fifty miles long by fifteen miles wide, well-grassed and watered, and affording one of the finest grazing and agricultural districts in the territory. The central part of the area enclosed by the circle of this river is occupied by Bald Mountain, from which the little streams rush down to the encircling river, around the northern flank; while many others from the south and east find their way to the Beaver-Head. This latter stream, rising in the southwest corner of Beaver-Head county, flows north to its junction with the Big-Hole, the most important part of its valley being thirty-five miles long and an average of six miles wide. Between these two rivers, for some twenty miles above their junction, is a level plain of good farming land that is easily susceptible of irrigation. There are many thrifty farmers and stock-growers along the immediate bottom lands, and more coming in every season.

The principal tributaries from the west are Rattlesnake, Willard, and Horse-Prairie creeks; those from the east are Red Rock and Blacktail Deer creeks—the last three having large valleys of excellent grazing and farming land.

Stinking Water river rises in the mountain at the south end of Madison county, and, running north, connects with the Jefferson a short distance below the junction of the Beaver-Head and Big-Hole. It has a valley about forty miles in length and of variable width, being separated into two parts by a short cañon directly opposite Virginia City. The upper portion, which is some fifteen to twenty miles long, and from one to five miles wide, is an excellent grazing section, and already there are large herds of common and thorough-bred stock being raised there. The upper valley is also well adapted to agriculture. The recent discoveries of immense coal beds at the extreme upper end of this district, has drawn much more than the usual attention to it the present season (1873), and the mines are fast proving valuable. Below the cañon, the valley is much wider than above, and affords a vast tract of most excellent farming land. Much of the lower valley is thickly settled, and enormous crops are yearly being produced. Apples, plums, and other fruits are successfully cultivated.

Where the three streams, Big-Hole, Beaver-Head, and Stinking Water, unite to form the Jefferson, there is a broad, level area, the greater part of which may be irrigated and made good farming land. And this point must become one of considerable importance as the territory increases in population, on account of the advantages of its position; for here must always be the junction of the roads up Beaver-Head and Stinking Water, down the Jefferson and over Deer Lodge Pass. No matter how much the general direction of traffic and travel may change, these must ever remain lines of travel so long as there is any passing north and south in this section. In coming down from the Deer Lodge Pass one is completely captivated by the extreme beauty of the valley, which has the appearance of a vast grass-waving meadow; and, reaching the banks of Big-Hole and Beaver-Head, with their heavy volumes of pure, limpid water rushing down, one can easily see how abundantly it is blessed for water privileges.

The valley of the Jefferson, for twenty-eight or

thirty miles below this point, will average, exclusive of the table-lands which flank it, from three to five miles wide. The supply of water is ample not only to irrigate the bottoms or valley proper, but also a large portion of the table-lands, which at some points expand to a width of eight or ten miles, but in other places form but mere strips. The stream, which is probably one hundred and twenty to one hundred and fifty feet wide and two feet deep, is fringed by a growth of cottonwood and willow, the former often of quite large size. The bordering mountains are clothed with a heavy growth of dark pines from their summits down to the sloping foot-hills; from this dark green border the pale, smooth meadow sweeps down in a graceful curve on each side, giving to the valley a soft, attractive beauty seldom seen. What must have been the delight of Lewis and Clark, the great explorers, as they traversed this beautiful valley, then doubtless teeming with herds of buffalo, elk, deer, and other wild game. More than sixty years ago they passed over it on their route through the wilderness. What a change! A nation has sprung into existence on that which was then only the home of the red man and wild beast. And in all probability, before another quarter of a decade the shrill whistle of the locomotive will be heard reverberating among its clustering mountains and echoing amid its meadows.

Madison river, rising in the region of hot-springs and geysers, near Yellowstone lake, runs in a northern direction to Gallatin City, where it unites its waters with those of the Jefferson and Gallatin to form the Missouri. It is worthy of remark that from the Beaver-Head to the Yellowstone there appears to be a succession of short mountain ranges, or high ridges, running north and south, with intervening valleys of greater or less width, one of which is traversed by the Stinking Water, another by the Madison, and a third by the Gallatin.

The valley of the Madison is separated into two parts by a short cañon east of Virginia City. Above this it extends about twenty miles, varying in width from two to five miles, and is flanked by a succession of beautiful terraces almost perfectly horizontal, and which extend for miles along the valley, leading gently down from the mountains to the river on each side. On the east side of the valley several wild, dismal-looking cañons give egress to wooded streams of considerable size, and afford almost unlimited means of irrigation.

Meadow creek, which joins the Madison at the upper end of the cañon, traverses a small valley of fine farming land. This valley well deserves its name, for it is covered with a dense carpet of nutritious grasses and many sparkling brooks. That part of the Madison valley below the cañon is some twenty-five to thirty miles long, and has an average width of six miles. The average width of the river is about eighty yards, with a swift current and a bed of bowlders and gravel. The soil is not exceeded in any country; and as an evidence of this, most of the valley is already occupied by settlers.

The Gallatin river is formed by two streams, called East and West Forks. The East Fork flows for some distance through a cañon which ceases about twenty miles from its junction with the other fork. From this point it flows in a northwesterly direction, being from fifty to sixty yards wide, with high and attractive banks. The bottom lands on the east and west sides have an average width of three miles, a large portion of which is now under cultivation. On the east side the bench-land, excellent pasturage, extends eastward eight miles to Mill creek, or the right fork of the Gallatin. Mill creek runs northwest through the city of Bozeman, and there connects with the East Fork. East Fork, coming from the hills northeast of Bozeman, flows in a westerly course for six or eight miles, thence northwest to its junction with West Fork. It is some forty or fifty yards wide, flowing swiftly, its banks being high and not subject to overflow. The immediate valley is from two to five miles wide, while on the south a low table-land, not more than fifteen or twenty feet above the bottoms, stretches out to the south, ascending with a gentle slope to the foot of the mountains. The supply of water is ample, and the facilities for irrigation excellent. This is one of the finest valleys of this section, the soil being good and the climate favorable, on which account it has attracted settlers, so that at this time it is mostly enclosed and under cultivation; and it is probable that ere long an encroachment will be made on the bordering plateau. The stream is fringed by a fine growth of cottonwood and aspen, except which there is no other timber in the valley, this being supplied from the mountains to the northwest.

Passing northward from the central part of the Jefferson, we enter the eastern central basin. This is drained by the Missouri river below the Three Forks, and above them by the lower tributaries of the Jefferson, the North Bowlder, South Bowlder, and Willow creeks. It is also traversed by the lower portion of the Madison and Gallatin rivers, which form a junction with the Jefferson in a fertile plain of considerable extent. It contains a large amount of arable land, with a climate comparable to that of Utah, and is about one hundred and fifty miles long north and south, by eighty east and west. Its five principal valleys are the following: the valley of the Three Forks, of North Bowlder, of the lower part of the Jefferson, of the Madison, and of the Gallatin, furnishing a larger amount of farming land than the basin of the Beaver-Head and tributaries.

The valley of the Missouri along this part of its course is narrow, but quite fertile, possessing a very favorable climate. It is watered on the east side by numerous small streams, which flow down from the

Belt mountains. The interior of the basin is traversed by several sharp and elevated ridges; the principal one, stretching from near the lower part of the Jefferson a little west of north, connects with the Rocky mountain range near the origin of Prickly-Pear creek. The North Bowlder runs along the western base of the ridge, through a fine and fertile valley, while west of it runs another ridge, separating its waters from those of White-Tail Deer creek. Both those ridges are clothed with a dense growth of pine timber of excellent quality.

Prickly-Pear and Ten-Mile creeks have each pretty valleys, which, though irregular and contracted at some points by the approaching ridges, at others expand into broad, open prairies, with surfaces smooth as a meadow. One of these beautiful openings is in the vicinity of Helena, the view out upon and over which is very fascinating to the lover of scenery. The valley is from five to fifteen miles wide, and twenty-five to thirty miles long. The raising of all kinds of vegetables has proven a perfect success, and wheat will average fifty-two bushels to the acre; indeed, *eighty-two* bushels have been raised upon a single, measured acre. The average yield of oats is over forty-five bushels per acre, and that of barley thirty-five. Wheat is sown in this valley as early as the last of February, though generally the first days of March, which speaks volumes for the climate. Currants, gooseberries, strawberries, and raspberries, and the hardier varieties of apples and pears, can be and have been very successfully grown. Snow does not generally set in until in December, and does not often fall in the valleys after March; it never falls to any great depth, seldom enough for good sleighing. This fact in regard to the fall of snow appears somewhat paradoxical to those who have never visited these mountain regions. They read and hear statements in regard to snow in the mountains fifteen and twenty feet deep, and then in the next breath are told that cattle can graze out all winter, the snow not being sufficient to prevent this. It must be acknowledged these statements do appear to be somewhat contradictory, yet both are true.

On the east side of the Missouri, in the bend which this river makes here from a north to a northeast course, are two or three valleys, which may be considered, in this connection, though not strictly, belonging to the southern section. North Deep creek, that rises in the Belt mountains and flows north to the Missouri, has a valley some forty or fifty miles in length, which averages about three in width. At one place, for a distance of fifteen or twenty miles, it widens out to an average of five miles, but at other points the spurs of the mountains close in upon it, rendering it quite narrow. South Deep creek gives a valley of twenty-five or thirty miles in length and four or five in width, at no point within this distance being less than two miles wide. Water sufficient to irrigate these valleys can be obtained from these creeks and their tributaries, and near the mouth of the latter any deficiency can be supplied from the Missouri. The soil is good, and considerable settlements have already been made.

NORTHERN SECTION. This section comprises all that part of the territory lying east of the Rocky mountains and north of the divide which separates the waters of the Missouri from those of the Yellowstone. It is an extensive region, stretching from east to west some three hundred and fifty or four hundred miles, and varying in width, north and south, from one hundred to one hundred and seventy-five miles, including the north part of Deer Lodge, all of Choteau, and most of Meagher and Dawson counties. With the exception of the portions occupied by Belt, Highwood, and Judith mountains south of the Missouri, and by Bear's Paw and Little Rocky mountains north, it is generally an open, treeless plain, gradually descending eastward, with an average slope of five feet to the mile. But this descent differs very materially in the portions east and west of Fort Benton, that part west to the foot of the mountains having an average descent of from twelve to fifteen feet per mile, while that east has an average of less than three feet, if the barometric measurements taken along this line are to be relied upon.

Along the east base of the Rocky mountains, from the British possessions south to Sun river, there is a strip of arable land about thirty miles in width, which is well watered by numerous little tributaries of Marias, Teton, and Sun rivers. The descent here being somewhat rapid, and these streams but a few miles apart, flowing in rather parallel lines, a large portion of this strip, which is about one hundred miles in length, can be irrigated and brought under cultivation. It is yet wholly unoccupied, except by roving Indian bands; consequently no experiments in farming have been made. The grass is very good, and the great buffalo herd of Eastern Montana, apparently fleeing before the Sioux, has, during the present year, been moving over into this region. The Marias river, after it enters upon the plains, runs through a deep channel, bordered in part by broad table-lands, and partly by long, sloping hills, a part of which, by the construction of long ditches, may be reached and irrigated and rendered suitable for agricultural purposes.

Teton river is over one hundred miles long; and its two branches, rising in the Rocky mountains west of the Teton, flow around this butte and unite at its east base. There is much excellent bottom-land in its valley, which varies from two to six miles in width.

Sun river, rising in the Rocky mountains west of Fort Shaw, runs east about seventy-five miles, passing by this fort, and emp'ies into the Missouri. It forms the northern boundary-line of Lewis and Clark county. The cultivable valley of this river is about three miles wide, the soil being of the very best quality. The stream is some sixty or seventy yards wide, and flows very swiftly, forming one of the handsomest mountain rivers in the West. There are as yet but few settlements, and these at and near Fort Shaw, on the Helena and Fort Benton road. The river empties into the Missouri thirty miles from the fort.

The valley of the Missouri, from the Three Forks to the mouth of Sun river, is very rich and fertile, varying from three to eight miles in width; but at some points the hills close in upon it, leaving but a narrow strip of bottom-land along the stream. The length of the valley between these points is about one hundred and fifty miles. It is tolerably well settled, the climate being mild, and the productions as varied as any portion of the territory. Wheat, oats, rye, barley, corn, and the usual vegetables, grow well and produce heavy crops, Helena receiving a large part of its supply of vegetables from this valley. Such fruits as apples, plums, cherries, currants, raspberries, and gooseberries, may be grown and matured here, the climate presenting no serious obstacle.

As a general thing, after leaving the rapid descent near the base of the mountains, and entering upon the broad, open plains, the rivers of this section run in deep channels, which like deep ditches traverse the plains, and are often for long stretches sunk from one hundred to one hundred and fifty feet below the surface.

On the south side of the Missouri, the most important basins within this section are those of the Judith and Musselshell rivers. The Judith basin, now thought of as a reservation for the Crow Indians, spreads out forty or fifty miles, and extends north and south about eighty miles. It is traversed its entire length by the Judith river, which has three principal tributaries—West Fork, South Fork, and Big-Spring creek, all having fine grazing and agricultural valleys of considerable extent. The Judith valley proper is about eighty miles long, and varies in width from one to four miles. The bordering regions, approaching the Missouri, assume that barren appearance to which the name of *Mauvaises Terres*, or "Bad Lands," has been applied, yet the surface is fair pasture. From the mouth of the cañon on Musselshell below Fort Howie, for twenty-five miles down, is a very fine farming country, with good soil and climate.

SOUTHEASTERN SECTION. This section includes the area within the territory drained by the far-famed Yellowstone and its numerous tributaries. Comparatively little is known in regard to its agricultural resources as yet, but the attention of settlers is now fast becoming turned to this great unknown region. The following account, written by Judge H. L. Hosmer, then of Virginia and now of California, and first published in the Helena HERALD, will perhaps be as interesting and accurate as any we could give :

"No continuous account of this valley from the cañon, twenty-five miles beyond Bozeman, to the mouth, a distance by the stream of eight hundred and twenty miles, has ever been published. For the first eighty miles, from the mouth of the cañon, the river is almost one continuous rapid, and numerous ledgy islands are scattered along, which furnish coverts for large flocks of ducks. The banks are generally abrupt, in many places precipitous, thickly covered with stunted pines. Occasional accumulations of *debris* spread out into small bottoms, covered with immense cottonwoods. The banks on each side rise gradually into lofty hills, but the vegetation is light. Long, high ranges of mountains approach the river on each side. The water here is pure and very transparent. The bends of the stream are long and straight reaches, where the eye can often follow it for six or eight miles. Dense thickets of willow grow along the margin and on the islands. The second day we came in sight of the vast ridge of yellow sandstone, from which the river derives its name. This ridge appears to be about three hundred feet high, and this part twenty miles long, the bluff it forms being precipitous, and the top covered with pines. The valley of the river here is greatly expanded, spreading out into alluvial bottoms six or eight miles wide, gradually rising into upland and foot-hills. The soil here is equal to that of the Gallatin; but the descent of the river is much less rapid than above, miles intervening without any perceptible inclination. The termination of this portion of the ridge is at an angle of the river, where it has worn a passage through the rock on each hand, exhibiting a sheer, bold precipice of stratified sandstone, very hard, and of deep ochre color. The river is quite shallow where it crosses this ledge, which stretches off on the southwest side in a straight line across the valley for twenty or thirty miles. The bottoms here are extensive, (between the ridge and river,) and are susceptible of high cultivation. There are frequently long groves of cottonwood. We passed through this marvellous ridge five or six times in travelling three hundred miles. In some places it follows the river for miles, casting its sombre shadow on the water. In others it is curiously eroded into resemblances of towers, castles, citadels, etc. At the terminus of the ridge, the river, increased to twice the size it has at the commencement by the contributions of the Rose-Bud, Clarke's Fork, and Big-Horn, is fully one mile wide and very deep. Its waters turbid, its banks low, it rolls an immense volume of water down undisturbed by a ripple, through large, spreading meadows beautified by occasional trees and carpeted with a thick growth of grass. With the exception of a few rapids, some of which are formidable, this is the general character of the scenery until we approach the mouth of Powder river. Here a sudden change takes place, and all at once we are ushered from the highest state of verdure to that of extreme, absolute desolation. Here commence the *Mauvaises Terres*, and from this point to its mouth the same general features characterize the scenery as those found along the Upper Missouri, intensified, if possible, by frequent views of long burnt plains, seamed with immense ravines, and dotted with enormous tables of baked clay. It is, without exception, the most horrible-looking country I ever saw. The hills and mounds of stratified clay along the bank of the river rise fifteen hundred feet, void of vegetation. The river is here a dark drab color, with shifting channels and numerous sandbars. Its clay banks for hundreds of miles exhibit on each side continuous veins of decomposed lignite. A railroad could easily be built along its course, except the one hundred and eighty miles from the mouth of Powder river downward. Above Powder river the obstructions are few and easily overcome. Three or four hundred miles would be through the largest and richest valley in Montana, yet unsettled, and not more than fifteen hundred or two thousand feet above the level of the sea."

The information gained by the recent North Pacific Railroad surveys, not yet published in a condensed form, tend to show that the valley of the Yellowstone, generally speaking, is the best adapted to agriculture of any portion of the territory, and only needs reclaiming from the possession of the hostile Indians to be flooded with settlers and miners. At present it is not a safe country in which to permanently locate, nor will be until the North Pacific Railroad is built and protected through it.

RESOURCES. Of the agricultural and mineral resources of the territory, a volume could be truthfully written in commendation; but it is not our purpose to give in this work more than a mere general notice of its prominent features. These are agriculture, stock-raising, and mining. The products of the land now under cultivation are sufficient to sustain a population of two hundred thousand; and the fine lands yet open to pre-emption and settlement cover an almost unlimited area. The timber supply of Montana is far beyond its own needs, and will one day prove an incalculable source of wealth. Grazing lands are everywhere to be found, and may fairly be said to be inexhaustible. Of stock of all kinds there are now in the territory several hundred thousand head, and the importation and breeding of thoroughbred cattle are now becoming as common as in the states. The raising of cattle costs no more here in Montana than the expense of herding and branding, and is one of the most profitable avocations that can be followed. The mineral resources of the territory are as yet almost unknown. There are over one thousand placer-mining camps now discovered and being worked profitably; and the silver and gold quartz interest is represented by not less than ten thousand recorded lodes. While a few of these are being profitably mined and the ore reduced here or shipped, the great proportion are the property of poor men, and are lying untouched for the want of capital to develop and work them. The annual gold yield of the entire territory, since 1864, will come not far from averaging ten million dollars; while the silver product, yet in its infancy, bids fair to soon annually exceed this sum. New discoveries of both gold and silver mines are yearly being made, and the methods for profitable reduction of ores are constantly being improved. The actual cost of living is not greatly above the cost of living in the western states, and the profits of labor and trade are greatly in excess.

PRINCIPAL CITIES AND TOWNS.

VIRGINIA—the only incorporated city in Montana, and the capital of Montana Territory—was given birth and prominence to principally by the discovery of Alder Gulch, on the east bank of which it is built. In the early days it drew to itself nearly the entire population of the territory, and for a long time was the chief commercial centre. In those *wild* days—when gold was taken out of the gulch by millions, and recklessly squandered by the devotees of the gaming-table and dance-house—the town presented a Babel of confusion in business as well as society. The former was conducted in an extravagant style, and the latter—well, the least said about it now the better; it was *loose*—extremely loose! Ruffians of the most desperate character roamed the streets and murdered each other "on sight," with impunity. The whole aim seemed to be to get money and spend it in riotous living and extravagance. But all evils have an end. So was this evil way of living brought to a close. With immigration, the establishment of courts, and the healthful action of the vigilantes, a better state of affairs was inaugurated. Business gradually sought its legitimate channels; society became purified; the "roughs" were either hanged or driven from the country, and the moral element began to thrive. Ten years have passed; the bulk of the gold has been taken out of Alder and carried away; the population has been divided with her sister cities, and from a city of over twelve thousand it has now less than one-half of that number. It is still a thrifty commercial centre, and there is yet more gold in the gulch than will be taken out for fifty years to come. Alder Gulch yields now, annually, nearly one million dollars, and is being worked its entire length—eleven miles. The fertile valleys and thrifty mining camps surrounding make a steady and increasing demand for the goods of her merchants, and thousands of tons are yearly shipped and sold. The capital of the territory, and the county-seat of Madison county, it is perhaps better known to the outside world than any other town in the territory. It has telegraphic and daily coach communication, and the United States Signal Observatory. The society of Virginia is equal, for refinement, sociability, and morals, to any in the older states. Two newspapers are published and well supported—THE MONTANIAN, a forty-eight column weekly, Geo. F. Cope, proprietor; steam-power and presses of the best make. It is an independent journal, ably and successfully conducted, and claims an actual circulation of fifteen hundred. THE MADISONIAN (just being started), Thomas Deyarmen, proprietor—a democratic weekly. Virginia has fine church and school advantages, and the usual conveniences of a city. It is one of the starting points for the National Park.

HELENA is the county-seat of Lewis and Clark county, and is recognized as the chief commercial metropolis of the territory. The discovery of gold in Last Chance Gulch, in 1864-5, gave it birth. It has some of the finest public and private buildings in the territory, and more than double the population of any other town in Montana. It has a Fair Association, large smithy works, public library, several churches, and private and public schools, among which latter is St. Vincent's Female Academy, a flourishing Catholic institution, which is doing great good. The city stands surrounded by rich gold and silver mines, and furnishes a market for the east and northeast sections of the territory. Burned to the ground twice by devastating fires, its citizens have again built it up in better style than before, and are every year adding much to its beauty and wealth. It has two daily and two weekly papers: The HERALD, Fisk Brothers, editors and publishers, is a republican journal of the most uncompromising type, and has fought its way through hard times, fire, and heavy party opposition, to the front rank. It claims the largest daily and weekly circulation in Montana. The GAZETTE, owned and edited by the "Gazette Publishing Company," is a democratic daily and weekly, and has for years been the leading organ of the party. It has withstood fire and financial disaster, and is to-day one of the best conducted journals in the mountains. Circulation about fifteen hundred for the weekly and five hundred for the daily. The scenery about Helena is attractive, and its society all that could be desired. It has telegraphic and daily coach communication, and is the central office for all Montana stage lines.

DEER LODGE CITY is the county-seat of Deer Lodge county, and has the handsomest location in the territory. It is the metropolis of the West Side of Montana; has telegraphic and daily coach communication, substantial public and private buildings, and a thrifty and growing population. The Territorial Penitentiary is here located, and adds largely to the architectural wealth of the town. Sixteen miles from the city is a cluster of thermal springs, said to contain wonderful medicinal properties. This point has been improved by the erection of a twelve-thousand-dollar hotel, bath-house, etc., and is a fashionable resort. Deer Lodge has two weekly newspapers: THE NEW-NORTH-WEST, republican, Jas. H. Mills, editor and proprietor; a fine circulation, and recognized as one of the most ably edited journals in the West. THE INDEPENDENT, Kerly, Smith, Hathaway & McQuaid, editors and proprietors, is the democratic organ of the West Side, and conducted both financially and editorially with ability and success.

BOZEMAN is the county-seat of Gallatin county, one of the, if not the finest agricultural districts in Montana. It is the eastern metropolis of the territory, and a prominent rival of Helena. It is also a starting point for the National Park, and, like Virginia, has a wagon road to its limits. In mercantile houses, private dwellings, church and school advantages, society, telegraphic and coach communication, and all that goes to make it a desirable place to reside, it is unsurpassed by any of its sisters. Its people are thrifty and go-ahead, and contribute largely to the wealth and enterprise of the Territory. It has a democratic weekly paper—THE COURIER, Jos. Wright, editor and proprietor, which has a fine support, and has done much towards making the city what it is. The Courier compares favorably, in appearance and ability, with its contemporaries, and has a good circulation.

MISSOULA, the county-seat of Missoula county, is, like Deer Lodge and Bozeman, on the direct route of the Northern Pacific Railroad. It is the trading centre of a vast area of rich agricultural lands, and one of the best localities in the territory. Its people are thrifty and enterprising, and have provided themselves with churches and schools, and fine private and public buildings. THE MISSOULIAN, edited by Frank Woody, Esq., is a lively democratic newspaper, and receives a good support from the people.

BANNACK is the county-seat of Beaver-Head county, and the pioneer city of Montana. It is located in the centre of a rich silver and gold district, and affords a market for a great portion of its county. The shipment and crushing of gold and silver ores from the Blue Wing and other districts, forms a large portion of its industry, and its people are steadily growing wealthy.

RADERSBURG, the county-seat of Jefferson county, is a sprightly agricultural and mining town of about five hundred inhabitants, and is steadily building up into prominence and wealth. Its county and private buildings are very creditable, and its people plucky and industrious. One of the best, if not *the* best, paying gold mines in the Territory—" The Keating"—is located on the hills two miles west of the town, and yields annually a profit of from seventy-five to eighty thousand dollars.

FORT BENTON, county-seat of Choteau county, the head of steam navigation of the Missouri river, one hundred and forty-five miles northeast from Helena, has about one hundred and fifty inhabitants.

DIAMOND CITY is thirty-five miles west of Helena, and the county-seat of Meagher county. Its principal resource is the rich placer gold mines surrounding it, which will yet last for years.

The territory has many other fine growing villages, mention of which, in this general description, is necessarily omitted. It has also much beautiful scenery—the Missouri river falls, Flathead lake, Bald mountain, Mount Powell, the hot springs in Deer Lodge, Madison, and Lewis and Clark counties, etc., etc.—a description of which would swell our volume to too great a size.

The principal Federal officers are:

BENJ. F. POTTS, Governor, Virginia.
JAS. E. CALLAWAY, Secretary, "
W. E. CHILD, Register of Land Office, Helena.
SOL. STAR, Receiver, Helena.
Capt. T. P. FULLER, Collector of Int. Revenue, Helena.
THOS. A. CUMMINGS, Collector of Customs, "
W. F. WHEELER, United States Marshal, "
M. C. PAGE, United States Dist. Attorney, Radersburg.
D. S. WADE, Chief Justice, Helena.
HIRAM KNOWLES, Associate Justice, Deer Lodge.
F. G. SERVIS.   "   "   Virginia.

Just the Paper for Families.

Filled with spicy reading, and the general news of the day carefully condensed.

Elegant illustrations, of which

LOWER FALLS OF YELLOWSTONE,

CASTLE GEYSER,

HOT CONE SPRING,

and the

CAÑONS OF THE YELLOWSTONE

in this volume are fair samples.

THE

Illustrated Christian Weekly

is a large twelve-page paper, and will be sent to any address one year for

TWO DOLLARS.

We shall be happy to send samples to any address free.

American Tract Society,
150 NASSAU ST., NEW YORK.

VIRGINIA BUSINESS DIRECTORY.

PATTON & LAMBRECHT,

WHOLESALE and Retail Grocers, Masonic Temple Building (stone fire proof), Wallace Street, Virginia. Dealers in every variety of Groceries, Liquors, Provisions, Miners' Tools, Hardware, Tinware, Queensware, Cutlery. Woodenwares, Iron, Steel, Horse Shoes and Horse Nails, and all kinds of Wagon Timbers, Sash, Window Glass, etc; also, Cast and Sheet Iron Stoves. Manufacture and repair Tinware, etc. National Park Tourists can find everything to make camp-life pleasant by applying to us for an outfit. Camp Stoves and Cooking Utensils of all descriptions.

HARRINGTON, BAKER & CO.,

WHOLESALE and Retail Dealers in Boots, Shoes, and Leather Findings, Virginia, and Bozeman, Montana. All styles, qualities and prices in Gents', Ladies' and Children's footwear. We are in constant receipt of new goods, and keep fully up to the times in styles and reduction of prices. Rubber Boots of the very best manufacture. Tourists' coarse Boots got up and on hand especially for National Park tramps. They can't give out, are easy, and just the thing. Give us a call.

RAYMOND BROTHERS,

AGENTS for the celebrated Sweepstakes Threshing Machine, the Buckeye Reaper and Mower. Dealers in Hay Rakes, Drills, Fanning Mills, Plows, Schutler Wagons, etc., etc., etc. Wholesale and Retail Dealers in Groceries, Japan and China Teas, China Rice, and a full line in the Grocery Trade. Outfitting store for National Park Tourists. Can Fruits of every variety. Canned Meats, Corn, Pickles, Chow-Chow, etc.

DR. L. DAEMS,

WHOLESALE and Retail Druggist and Apothecary, keeps constantly on hand Drugs, Chemicals, Perfumery, Fancy Articles, etc. Also keeps constantly on hand a complete assortment of Patent Medicines, at the City Drug Store, Wallace Street, Virginia City, Montana Ter. Special attention paid to compounding Prescriptions.

"O. K. STABLES,"

T. J. FARRELL, Proprietor. Coach to the Geysers. Pack and Saddle Horses and Mules furnished and equipped at a moment's notice. This Stable has fine Buggies and Carriages for hire at reasonable rates. Saddle Horses of the best gait and disposition. Hay, Grain, and good care of Horses left in my charge is a specialty. Stock of all kinds bought and sold. National Park Tourists can find a good outfit by applying at the "O. K. Stables," either for wagon accommodation or horse-back riding.

WM. G. PFOUTS,

WHOLESALE Grocer, Virginia, Montana. A full assortment of all goods in the line, and prices as low as any other house.

VIRGINIA BUSINESS DIRECTORY.

D. W. TILTON. TILTON & BARBER, O. B. BARBER.

POST-OFFICE Building. Books, Stationery, Wall Paper, Picture and Picture Frames, Notions and Toys, National Park Stereoscopic Views, and in fact, anything in the full line. Tobacco and Cigars at wholesale and retail. Pipes, Cigar Cases, and Holders. Low prices and good goods in everything.

D. F. OGDEN, L.D.S.,

DENTIST, Virginia City, M. T. All work pertaining to the profession executed in the best possible manner. Purvine's Patent Plate for Artificial Teeth. Charges reasonable. All work warranted.

LUMBER, LATH AND SHINGLES.

I KEEP constantly on hand at my yard—one door above Hussey, Dahler & Co.'s Bank, Virginia City, also at my mills—White and Red Pine Lumber, suitable for building or mining purposes. Lath and Shingles, of superior quality, at the lowest market price. Live Stock, Grain and Produce taken in exchange. Orders promptly filled, and goods delivered when desired. WILLIAM THOMPSON. Herndon & Donaldson, Agents.

CHRIS. KIBLER,

METROPOLITAN Meat Market, has again taken charge of this Market. Everything in the meat line will be found at the Metropolitan of the most choice character, and it will be sold at living rates. The shop will be supplied at all times with Beef, Veal, Pork and Mutton. Chris. is himself again at the old stand, and will be happy to see all his old customers and as many new ones as may see fit to bestow their patronage.

HERNDON & DONALDSON,

BUILDERS, will contract for work in the city or country. Keep on sale Doors and Sash; also, Building Paper, a thick, solid pasteboard, a good substitute for plastering, at half the cost. We keep a Lumber Yard in connection with our shop. All our work is warranted to give satisfaction.

THE OLD RELIABLE GOHN'S

MEAT Market (two doors below Post-Office corner), Virginia City, Montana (in the stand of the Old Metropolitan Market). Geo. Gohn wishes to inform the public that he has opened a Meat Market at the above stand, and will sell Beef, Veal, Pork, Mutton by the carcass, quarter, or cut, at fair living rates. He has not gone into the business to sell only his own stock, but intends to remain in the butchering business permanently. He intends keeping a full market of Meats of the best quality, at all times, and wholesale or retail. Customers will be promptly and fairly dealt by. Give me a call.

JAMES G. SPRATT,

ATTORNEY and Counselor-at-Law, Virginia City, Montana.

HENRY N. BLAKE,

LATE U. S. and District Attorney, Attorney and Counselor-at-Law, Virginia City, M. T. Will practice in all the courts of Montana.

SAMUEL WORD,

ATTORNEY-AT-LAW, Virginia City, M. T. Will practice in all the courts of Montana.

B. F. POTTS,

ATTORNEY and Counsellor-at-Law, Virginia City, Montana.

JAMES E. CALLAWAY,

ATTORNEY-AT-LAW, Virginia City, Montana. Will practice in all the courts in the Territory and the Land Office at Helena. Office adjoining office of the Secretary of the Territory.

THOMAS WHITE,

CAPITAL Barber Shop, next door to the Post-office. Hot and Cold Baths. None but artists in their profession employed. Prices reduced to suit the march of civilization and the irrepressible events of the day. Tourists to the National Park are especially invited to come in and see me.

THE VIRGINIA BREWERY.

ESTABLISHED 1863. H. S. Gilbert, Proprietor. Lager Beer of a very superior quality always kept on hand, and delivered to order at any point desired within the county. Also Malt, Hops, and Brewers' Supplies constantly on hand and for sale at reasonable prices. Lager Beer at from $5 to $8 per keg, according to size. The Virginia Brewery is without doubt the most complete establishment of the kind west of the Missouri river, having been built at an expense of twenty thousand dollars in gold. The Brewer now employed by me is a gentleman of much experience, both in Europe and America, and has a thorough knowledge of the business, as the superior quality of Beer turned out abundantly attests. Thankful for past favors, a countinuance of patronage is hereby solicited. ☞ Parties calling at the Brewery will always find attention, and be supplied with the best Beer on tap. H. S. GILBERT.

HARRY WARMINGTON'S NEW STORE.

CALL in for all kinds of Gents' Furnishing Goods, Ladies' Dress and Dry Goods, Notions of the Trade, &c., &c. Having just bought an entire new and fresh Stock of Goods, the public will find it to their advantage to call. No "Old Clothes" on hand. Everything new and stylish. Prices cut right "down to bed rock."

WILLIAM DOUGLAS,

DEALER in Fancy Groceries, Fancy Goods, Fruits, Confections, Toys, and Notions. The best place to buy in the city. Square dealing and small profits.

VIRGINIA STABLES,

HENRY WERKEN, Proprietor. I would respectfully notify the Public that I am still keeping Stable at the old stand, Lower Wallace street, and invite the patronage of those who would like their Stock well taken care of at very reasonable prices. LIVERY—A good stock of Buggy and Saddle Horses constantly on hand and to let. ☞ I am now the sole owner of the Wigwam Lumber Mill, and am prepared to furnish any description of Lumber at short notice, and at prices to suit the times. HENRY WERKEN.

J. F. STOER,

LOWER Wallace Street, Virginia City, Montana. Wholesale and Retail Dealer in Groceries, Liquors, Tobaccos, and Produce of all Kinds. Keeps a well-assorted stock always on hand. The Farmers' and Miners' Trade made a specialty. Buys Wheat, Oats, Barley, Pork, Flour, Potatoes, Butter, and Produce of all kinds, and pays the very highest Market Price for the same. He is at his old stand. Give him a call before buying your Goods or selling your Grain or Produce.

GILMER & SALISBURY,

SUCCESSORS to Wells, Fargo & Co. Stage Line carrying the U. S. Mail and Wells, Fargo & Co's Express. Offices at Virginia, Helena, Deer Lodge, Missoula, and all other principal towns in the Territory. Every Convenience for Passenger Travel. Our Line extends throughout Montana, Utah, Idaho, and Nevada.

JNO. PFIEL,

WAGON-MAKER and Repairer, is at all times ready to attend to those desiring his services. Shop on Lower Wallace street. All work warranted to be done as represented. Charges reasonable.

EUREKA SALOON,

J. WIMMER, Proprietor. The only really first-class Saloon and Club Room in the city. This fine establishment occupies three floors, is carpeted from top to bottom, and embellished in good taste. Nothing but first-class Wines, Liquors, and Cigars kept in the house. Guests can rely on good treatment and courteous attention.

NORTH PACIFIC BILLIARD HALL,

J. WELLS, Proprietor. Next door to the Clasbey House. Good Tables and Fine Bar Stock. Ample arrangements for all the Social Games. Drop in and see me.

CAPITAL SALOON,

THOMAS McGARRY, Proprietor. "Headquarters for the Boys." Fine Liquors, Cigars, and Lager. A good Cl b Room attached. Polite attention to Customers, and nothing left undone to make things pleasant. No cheap Liquors kept. "One man's money is as good as another's" is my motto.

JOHN SPIKER,

CALIFORNIA Bakery and Saloon, Wallace street, Virginia City, M. T., has constantly on hand Pies, Bread, Liquors, Beer, Cider, Cigars, &c., &c., &c.

MONTANA BREWERY & BAKERY.

JOHN MANNHEIM, at his Old Stand on Wallace street, Virginia City, M. T. Families and Bachelors will find it to their advantage to go to his popular place for their Bread, Pies, Cakes, and all kinds of Confectioneries. The Saloon is always supplied with the best of Liquors, Wines, and Cigars. Lager Beer, from the celebrated Montana Brewery, always on hand, which will be delivered to all parts of the city and county, either in bottles or kegs.

H. A. PEASE,

WATCHMAKER and Jeweler, and Dealer in American Watches and Clocks, Virginia City, Montana. Jewelry manufactured from Native Gold.

H. BRUNDAGE,

GUNSMITH and Machinist. Guns, Pistols, Ammunition, and Sporting Material.

THEXTON & CO.,

BLACKSMITHS and Machinists, Virginia, M. T. Horse, Mule, and Cattle Shoeing. Special attention given to Miners' Tools. Job Work and Repairing neatly and promptly done. Engines and Boilers repaired, and all Classes of Work pertaining to Machinery performed in a workmanlike manner. Star Livery Stable adjoining the shop, will be found a large and well-appointed Livery and Feed Stable, under the proprietorship of George Thexton, who keeps a constant supply of Grain and Hay. Farmers and others will find this a desirable place for stock. Prices to suit the times.

JULIUS KRAEMER,

HARNESS and Saddle Maker. All kinds of Saddles, Whips, Bridles, Cantinas, Cinches, &c. Repairing at reasonable rates. Call. Wallace street.

J. B. CROCKETT,

HARNESS and Saddle Maker, and Dealer in all kinds of Saddles, Harness, Whips, Combs, Brushes, and Horse Clothing generally, at Wholesale and Retail. Tourists and others can buy cheaper than the articles can be rented. Wallace street.

A. LACROIX,

BOOT and Shoe Maker and Repairer. Fashionable fine French Calf Boots made to order, and a Perfect Fit warranted. Boots and Shoes of all kinds made or repaired in the very best Style, and at as Low Prices as any Shop in the Territory. None but superior workmen employed.

MEYER & KOERNER,

TEN Pin Alley Saloon. Farwell's Old Stand. The Alleys are always kept in fine order, and the Bar supplied with the best Brands of Liquors and Cigars to be had in the market. We have put prices right down to States' rates, and at the same time keep only the best quality of stock. 12½ cents for Drink or a Cigar. Call.

PONEY SALOON,

CORNER of Wallace and Jackson streets. The Bar Stock is unexceptionably the best in the Territory, and the House has appointments superior to any west of the Missouri river. A fine Club Room in connection. "Kentucky Favorite" a specialty. Every courtesy extended.　　　　　　　　　　　JNO. MAHAN & CO.

A. J. ROSENSTINE,

KEEPS a full Line of Dry Goods, Carpets, Oil Cloths, Matting, Ladies' Goods, Millinery Goods, and everything in the Dry Goods Line. He has put Prices down to suit the dull times, and is determined to sell goods lower than ever sold before in the market. Special attention paid to Farmers and people from the country.

E. H. BARTLETT,

BLACKSMITH, Horseshoer, and Machinist, is always ready to accommodate the wants of the people. Machines repaired, Oxen, Mules, and Horses Shod in the best manner, and Prices reasonable. What more can you ask? None but superior workmen employed. Tourists will call around and get their Baggage Animals heeled before going to the Geysers.

THE MONTANIAN.

STEAM Power Printing Establishment, Virginia City, M. T. Geo. F. Cope, Proprietor. Terms of the Weekly Montanian, $6.00 per year in advance. All kinds of Job and Book Work executed to order. Patronage respectfully solicited. Publication Office, Jackson Street, one door from Wallace.

CLASBEY HOUSE.

GEO. H. CLARK, Proprietor. This old, well-known, and favorite Virginia Hotel has been entirely refitted and furnished for the reception of guests. Good rooms, good beds, good fare, and fair prices. We make the comfort of our guests a study, and spare no pains to render the house deservedly popular with the public. Overland coach stops at and departs from this Hotel.

CRESCENT HOTEL.

ROBT. CONWAY, Proprietor. A first-class Hotel, with better Rooms and Beds than any other house in the city. Tourists to the National Park, and travelers and visitors generally will find this Hotel a desirable stopping place while in the city. Coaches arrive at and depart from the Crescent daily. Table supplied with the best the market affords. Charges moderate.

OLIVE BRANCH SALOON

KEEPS the best Brands of Wines, Liquors. and Cigars. Virginia City, M. T. next to Court House. Geo. W. Todd. Established 1864; 1873.

THE MADISONIAN.

VIRGINIA City, Montana. Thos. Deyarmon, Proprietor. Terms, $5 per year, in advance. Job Work done with neatness and dispatch. Subscriptions and Job Work solicited.

J. L. CORBETT,

CIVIL Engineer, Virginia City, M. T., will attend to calls in his line with promptness and attention. Office at Daem's Drug Store.

N. T. BUTLER,

MANUFACTURING Jeweler, Virginia City, Montana. dealer in Howard Watches, Elgin Watches. Waltham Watches, Seth Thomas Clocks, Seth Thomas, Son & Co. Clocks, Spectacles, etc., etc. Established, 1863.

PHOTOGRAPHS.

VIRGINIA City Photograph Gallery, Jackson Street, Virginia City, M. T. Mr. O. C. Bundy and lady are now prepared to take Pictures in all of the Latest Styles, and at the most reasonable rates. Parties will find at our Reception Room an artistic and varied selection of Mountain Views! Those desiring Pictures are invited to call soon. ☞ Rooms formerly occupied by Thrasher.

HENRY ELLING,

BANKER and dealer in Gold, Silver, Bullion and Dust, Virginia City, M.T. All kinds of Bankable Securities. Bills of Exchange on all principal cities of the U. S. and Europe.

I. STRASBURGER,

DEALER in Staple and Fancy Dry Goods, of every variety and description. An examination and comparison of stock and prices is respectfully solicited. Orders from the country given special attention.

ARMSTRONG & JOHNSON,

SUCCESSORS of Henry Elling, dealers in Clothing and Furnishing Goods, Hats, Caps, California Blankets, Canvas and Hydraulic Hose, for Mining purposes. Also, a large assortment of Rubber Clothing, &c. Tourist's Outfitting Store. Great Bargains offered to Wholesale Buyers. W. P. Armstrong. M. D. Johnson.

C. L. DAHLER,

SUCCESSOR to Hussey, Dahler & Co., Banker, Virginia City, Montana, dealer in Gold Dust, Coin, and Exchange. Collections promptly attended to on all points in this Territory and the States. Exchange drawn in Currency or Coin, on the following Correspondents: Messrs. Kountze Brothers, 12 Wall St., New York. First National Bank Utah, Salt Lake City. Utah. Warren, Hussey & Co., Corrinne, Utah. Bank of California, San Francisco, California. First National Bank, Deer Lodge, Deer Lodge, Montana. First National Bank, Bozeman, Bozeman, Montana. Fox, Lyster & Roe, Helena, Montana. Exchange drawn on the Principal Cities of Europe.

E. J. WALTER,

OVERLAND Clothing Store, keeps constantly on hand a large and well selected Stock of Gents' and Boys' Clothing, Hats, Caps, Gents' Furnishing Goods, Blankets, etc., which he offers at prices to defy competition. Tourists to the National Park will find it to their advantage to call on me before fitting out. I have a general supply store.

W. W. MORRIS,

WHOLESALE and Retail Dealer in Drugs, Chemicals, Patent Medicines, Paints, Oils, Window Glass, Stationery, Perfumery, Toilet and Fancy Articles. Coal Oil Lamps and Fixtures. And everything usually kept in a first-class Drug house. All of which I offer to the trade as low as they can be bought in the Territory. Physicians' prescriptions carefully compounded at all hours.

E. U. DRIGGS & CO.,

DEALERS in Stoves, Tin and Sheet-Iron Ware, Hardware and Queens Ware. Camping Stoves and outfits of all styles, and at all prices, to suit Tourists and others. Be sure and call. Stonewall Building, Virginia City.

HELENA BUSINESS DIRECTORY.

MURPHY, NEIL & CO.,
HELENA, Montana, Dealers in Staple and Fancy Groceries, Provisions, Wines, Liquors, Cigars, at Wholesale and Retail.

DR. THOS. REECE,
PHYSICIAN and Surgeon. Office, No. 42 St. Louis Hotel, Helena, Montana.

L. B. WELLS,
WHOLESALE and Retail Dealer in Millinery Goods, Main Street, Helena, M. T. The particular attention of Ladies is called to our elegant assortment of new and fashionable Dress Goods, Hats, Bonnets, Flowers, Plumes, Ornaments, &c. Send for Price List.

W. G. BAILEY,
MAIN Street, Helena, M. T., Dealer in Ladies' and Gents' Fine Gold Stem Winding Watches. Heavy American Silver Cases, Howard, Elgin and American Watch Co. Movements, Swiss and English Watches of all kinds. A fine assortment of new styles of Gold Chains, Ladies' Pearl Cut Coral, Moss Agate and Gold Enameled Sets of Jewelry, and Bracelets of the latest patterns; also, a fine assortment of Solid Silver Ware.

MAIN ST. MEAT MARKET, Helena, Montana.
WILLIAMS & PHILLIPS, Proprietors. Fresh and Salt Meat of all kinds. No poor Stock killed. Our Patrons can rely on getting the very best Meats the City or County affords. Prices as low as any other market in town.

NARROW GAUGE SALOON,
MAIN Street, Helena, M. T. DENNIS SHEEHY, Proprietor. Fine Wines, Liquors and Cigars. Headquarters for everybody. Next door to Pacific Stables.

JNO. B. LeBEAU,
MANUFACTURING Jeweler, and Dealer in Fine and Common Gold and Silver Watches, Main Street, Helena, M. T. Jewelry made to order, and warranted to be as represented. A good stock of Watches and Jewelry always on hand. Prices to suit the times.

UNION BREWERY,
MAIN Street, Helena, M. T., B. BINZEL, Proprietor. Lager Beer by the Keg and Gallon.

HELENA BUSINESS DIRECTORY. 121

KIYU'S SALOON,

NO. 3 Wood Street, J. C. SPANGLER, Proprietor, Helena, M. T. The oldest established House in Helena.

J. H. Shober.   T. J. Lowry.
SHOBER & LOWRY,
ATTORNEYS at Law and Collecting Agents, Helena, Montana, practice in all Courts in Montana Territory.

R. LAWRENCE,
ATTORNEY at Law.   Office, on Main Street, over Feldberg's Store.

DR. J. S. GLICK,
HELENA, Montana.

BENJ. ROBINSON, M. D.,
HELENA, Montana.

THE RUSSIAN MEDICATED BATHS

ARE a sure cure for Rheumatism, Mountain Fever and all Skin disease. They can be had at Dr. E. FRANK'S Tonsorial Rooms, Main Street, Helena, M. T. The only first-class establishment in Helena.

HENRY FRANK,

TAILOR, Main Street, Helena, Montana. Making and Repairing on short notice' and in a style surpassed by no other shop in the Territory. Give me a call.

CITY PHOTOGRAPH GALLERY,

E. H. TRAIN, Proprietor, No. 48 Main Street, Helena, M. T. All the latest styles of Pictures executed in the highest style of the art. National Park and other Mountain Scenery for sale. Satisfaction guaranteed.

UNIONVILLE SALOON,

PATRICK QUINN, Proprietor, next door to Travis' Stables, Main St., Helena M. T. Fine Wines, Liquors and Cigars.

SOL STAR,
NOTARY Public, Helena, Montana.

E. W. TOOLE,
ATTORNEY at Law, Helena, Montana.

6

THE FIRST NATIONAL BANK OF HELENA.

FINANCIAL Agent of the U. S., and Approved Depository for U. S. Disbursing Officers. Directors—S. T. Hauser, President; S. M. Hall, Vice-Pres.; D. C. Corbin, Cashier; T. H. Kleinschmidt, Ass't Cashier; W. B. Dance, Moses Moore, F. L. Worden, Jno. E. Blaine, Benj. Stickney, Jr.

We buy and sell all kinds of Local Securities, Gold Dust, Gold Coin, and Gold and Silver Bullion. Funds transferred by Telegraph to New York, San Francisco, St. Louis, and Omaha. Especial care and attention given to making Collections in this and adjoining Territories. Interest allowed on Time Deposits.

Correspondents—Clarke, Dodge & Co., and Austin Corbin, New York; St. Louis National Bank, St. Louis; Bank of California, San Francisco; Omaha National Bank, Omaha.

OUR SAMPLE ROOM,

CORNER Wood and Main Streets, Helena, M T. The oldest and only first-class Saloon in the Territory. Superior in all of its departments, and equal to any west of the Missouri River. I. MARKS, Proprietor.

FRANK BARTOS,

MANUFACTURING Jeweler, Helena, M. T., dealer in Clocks, Watches, Chains, and a full line of Jewelry. Also, Manufacturer of Fine Cigars. Orders promptly attended to.

HELENA BREWERY,

HORSKY & Kenck, Proprietors, Main Street, Helena, M. T. Ale and Beer delivered to order of customers. Everything on first-class principles. Try our Beer.

SAINT LOUIS BREWERY,

MAIN Street, Helena, M. T., A. Gerhauser, Proprietor, wholesale and retail dealer in Beer, Porter and Ales. Goods delivered to order. Nothing but the best materials used.

THE CENTRE OF ATTRACTION.

CALL and examine the Fine and Fashionable Clothing at J. Feldberg's. Also, the finest and best selected stock of Gents' Furnishing Goods in the city. Boys' and Youths' suits, Hats, Boots, and Shoes, Trunks and Valises, at Wholesale and Retail. ☞ Don't forget the place, opposite the First National Bank.

TEN-MILE BREWERY,

KESSLER & Miller, Proprietors. First and best quality of Beer, Ale and Porter. We have the best and most extensive Brewery and Hall in Montana. Goods delivered.

ERWIN & TODD, GROCERS,

BRIDGE Street, Helena, Montana. Groceries, Provisions, and a full line of everything in the trade. Low prices, quick returns, good goods, and fair dealing, are the features of this house.

W. W. JOHNSON,

DEPUTY Mineral Land Surveyor, Helena, M. T. Surveys of Quartz and Placer Mines a specialty. All business in my line promptly attended to.

HELENA BUSINESS DIRECTORY. 123

THE PEOPLE'S NATIONAL BANK

OF Helena, Main Street, Helena, Montana. Paid in Capital, $100,000; authorized Capital, $500,000. Geo. W. Fox. President. C. J. Lyster, Cashier. Directors: William Roe, Henry Klein, Nick Millen, P. T. Williams, Alex. II. Beattie, C. J. Lyster, Geo. W. Fox.

HARTWELL & CO., HELENA, M. T.,

WHOLESALE and Retail Lumber Dealers. Lumber in all shapes, dressed or in the rough. Shingles, Lath, Sash, Doors and Blinds, and building timber on hand and to order. The most extensive Lumber Market in the Territory. All work promptly attended to.

DAILY GAZETTE.

PUBLISHED every morning, except Monday, by the Gazette Publishing Company. Publication office, Gazette Granite Building, Bridge Street. Terms—City Subscribers, delivered by Carrier, per month, $3 00; by Mail, one copy, one month, $3 00; one copy, three months, $6 00; one copy, six months, $12 00. Weekly Gazette, $5 per year, in advance. Advertisements solicited.

THE HELENA HERALD,

DAILY and Weekly. Fisk Bros., Editors and Publishers, Helena, M. T. Publication office, Granite Building, Main Street. Terms—City Subscribers, delivered by Carrier, per month, $3 00; by Mail, one copy, one month, $3 00; one copy, three months, $6 00; one copy, six months, $12 00. Good Job Office.

JOS. MAGEE.   ## MAGEE & CO.,   G. E. McKIERNAN.

WHOLESALE Wines, Liquors, Cigars, Bar Glassware, etc., Main Street, two doors above St. Louis Hotel, Helena, Montana.

CHAS. MAYN & CO.,

WHOLESALE and Retail Dealers in Groceries, Liquors, Tobacco, etc., Main Street, Helena, M. T. Allow us to call your attention to our large assortment of Staple and Fancy Groceries, on which we offer great inducements to purchasers. Call on us, before purchasing elsewhere.

CHAS. MAYN & CO

W. F. SANDERS,

ATTORNEY and Counselor-at-Law, will practice in all Courts of Record in Montana. Helena City, M. T.

COSMOPOLITAN HOTEL,

SAM. SCHWAB, Proprietor, Helena, Montana. This Hotel is centrally located, and is the cheapest and best house west of St. Louis.

N. H. WEBSTER,

WHOLESALE and Retail Dealer in Tobaccos, Cigars, Snuff, Pipes, etc., and all descriptions of Fine Cut and Plug Chewing and Smoking Tobacco, Playing Cards and Ammunition, Travis Building, Helena, Montana.

A. LAVENBERG & CO.,

IMPORTERS of and Dealers in Staple and Fancy Dry Goods, Millinery, Straw Goods and Trimmings, Embroideries, Laces, Ladies' and Children's Shoes, Notions, etc. Carpets, Oil Cloths, Matting, Wall Paper, Window Curtains, Cornices, etc., etc. Ladies' and Children's Cloaks Shawls, Underwear, Hosiery, Gloves, etc., etc. Orders from the country solicited and promptly filled. Main Street, Helena, Montana.

MAGNOLIA HOTEL,

MAIN Street, Helena, M. T. (foot of Broadway), Christian Kenck, Proprietor, one of the oldest and most popular Hotels in Helena. First-class Board and Rooms. Charges reasonable.

J. H. MING & CO.,

BOOKSELLERS, Stationers, and Dealers in Fancy Goods and Notions, Helena, M. T. John H. Ming. Chas. K. Wells.

W. E. Cullen. CULLEN & COMLY, Harry R. Comly.

ATTORNEYS-AT-LAW, Helena, M. T, will practice in all the Courts of the Territory and in the United States Land Office. Office opposite Helena Library Rooms, in Holter & Brother's Brick Building.

D. MORRIS,

IMPORTER and Dealer in Havana and Dom stic Cigars, Tobaccos, Notions, Cutlery, Candies, Nuts, California and Oregon Fruits, etc., Main Street, Helena (one door above Ming & Co.), Montana, Territory.

R. S. HALE,

WHOLESALE and Retail Dealer in Drugs, Chemicals, Paints, Oils, Window Glass, and Dye Stuffs, Main Street, Helena, Montana.

J. T. WARD,

BOOKSELLER, Stationer, and Dealer in Fancy Goods and Notions, the latest Books, Music, Song Books, Newspapers and Periodicals, Helena, M. T.

OFFICE OF SANDS BROTHERS,

DEALERS in Dry Goods, Furnishing Goods, and Carpets, No. 48 Main Street, Helena, Montana. A. Sands, Helena. J. Sands, New York.

OTTO SWANSON,

MERCHANT Tailor, Main Street, Helena, Montana. Having leased the building formerly occupied by R. F. May, and being in receipt of a large assortment of Fine Cloths and Cassimeres, I am prepared to execute orders for Gentlemen's Clothing in the Latest Styles! Perfect Fits and satisfaction guaranteed. OTTO SWANSON.

INTERNATIONAL HOTEL, HELENA, M. T.

THIS Commodious Hotel is First Class in all its appointments to suit the most fastidious, and also at prices to warrant satisfaction.

HOYT & BRO.,

DEALERS in Groceries, Farm Produce, Liquors, Wines, Cigars, &c., 60 Main Street, Helena, Montana. E. M. Hoyt, P. Hoyt.

T. C. GROSHON,

WHOLESALE Dealer in Bourbon Whiskies, Brandies, Wines, Gins, &c., Main street, Helena, M. T.

J. R. BOYCE & CO.,

DEALERS in Dry Goods, Carpets, Ladies' and Children's Shoes, etc.. Bentley's Block, Main Street, Helena, Montana. J. R. Boyce, Sr. J. R. Boyce, Jr.

J. A. CREIGHTON & CO.,

FORWARDING and Commission Merchants, will give their prompt and personal attention to the receiving and forwarding of freights to Montana and Idaho. Freight promptly forwarded at the lowest going rates. Mark consignments "Care J. A. C. & Co.," Corrinne, Utah. Principal Offices: Helena, Montana. Corrinne, Utah.

J. A. Creighton.   Geo. S. Kennedy.

CHARLES LEHMAN,

COMMISSION Merchant, Dealer in Groceries, Wines, Liquors, Hardware and Farmers' Produce, Fire Proof Stores, No. 70 Main Street, Helena City, Montana. I have two large Fire Proof Stores, and pay especial attention to Storage and Commission.

LOEB & BROTHER,

IMPORTERS and Jobbers of Clothing, Dry Goods, Boots, Shoes, Hats, Fancy Goods, &c., Granite Block, Main Street, Helena, Montana.

McLEOD & JACK,

MAIN-STREET, Helena, M. T. Hardware and Stove Store. We would respectfully inform our numerous friends and patrons that we have the Largest and most Complete Assortment of Goods in our line ever brought to the Territory, which we offer at the lowest prices at Wholesale and Retail. Tin and Sheet Iron Pipe and all kinds of Tinware manufactured on short notice. W. T. McLeod. Wm. Jack.

GANS & KLEIN.

THE Emporium of Fashionable Clothing! The Largest Stock in the Territory. Gents' Underwear and Furnishing Goods. California Blankets, Duck Hose, Miners' Suits and India Rubber Goods. Boots and Shoes, Hats and Caps. Stationery and Yankee Notions. The Trade is respectfully invited to an examination of our Goods and Prices. Gans & Klein, Main Street, Helena, M. T. Louis Gans, New York. Henry Klein, Helena, Montana.

E. G. MACLAY & CO.,

RECEIVING, Forwarding, and Commission Merchants, General Freighters, and Government Contractors. Unequalled facilities in the way of Transportation and Storage. Principal Office, Helena, Montana.

DEER LODGE BUSINESS DIRECTORY.

MURPHY, HIGGINS & CO.,

DEER Lodge, M. T., dealers in Staple and Fancy Groceries, Provisions, Wines, Liquors, Cigars, Miners' and Ranchmen's Supplies generally. Sole Agents for the Celebrated "Chicken Cock" Miller Whiskey.
John T. Murphy. W. W. Higgins. Samuel Neel.

OSBORN & DENNEE,

WHOLESALE Grocers, and Dealers in Rubber and Leather Boots, Deer Lodge, Montana.
J. S. Osborn. W. McK. Dennee.

WM. H. WEIMAR & CO.,

WHOLESALE and Retail Grocers, Dealers in Wines, Liquors, Tobacco and Cigars, Deer Lodge, M. T. Miners' Hydraulic Hose and Quicksilver a Speciality.

Dan. Gamer. Fred. Gamer.

GAMER BROTHERS,

SUCCESSORS to John P. Fink & Co., Dealers in Boots and Shoes, Leather and Shoemakers' Findings, Deer Lodge, Montana Ter.

FIRST NATIONAL BANK

OF Deer Lodge. W. A. Clark, President; R. W. Donnell, Vice-President; S. E. Larabie, Cashier, draw Exchange on all the principal Cities of the World. New York Correspondents, Donnell, Lawson & Co., No. 4 Wall Street.

F. B. MILLER,

DEER Lodge City, Montana, Wholesale and Retail Dealer in Farmers', Miners' and Mechanics' Tools, Builders' Hardware, Iron, Steel, Nails, Queensware, Mowers and Reapers, Singer's Sewing Machines, Mount Vernon Duck, and Hose of all sizes. General Manufacturer of Hydraulic Pipe, Copper, Zinc, Sheet Iron and Tinware. Buck & Wright's Parlor, Heating and Cooking Stoves.

WILLIAM WOODWARD,

POST-OFFICE Store, Deer Lodge, Wholesale and Retail Dealer in Stationery. Cutlery, Notions, Cigars and Tobaccos. Newspapers and Periodicals for sale. Orders from the Country promptly attended to.

SCOTT HOUSE,

DEER Lodge City, Montana. Sam'l Scott, Proprietor. First-class fare, elegant rooms and beds, and polite attention to guests. The patronage of the resident and travelling public is respectfully solicited.

THE NEW NORTH-WEST,

PUBLISHED every Saturday at Deer Lodge, Montana. James H. Mills, Editor and Publisher. Terms—payable invariably in advance: One year, $6 00; Six months, $3 50; Three months, $2 00.

WEEKLY INDEPENDENT.

J. C. KERLEY, M. D. Hathaway, Addison Smith. Hugh M'Quaid. Kerley, Smith, McQuaid & Co., Publishers and Proprietors. Rates of Subscription: One copy one year, $6 00; six months, $4 00; three months, $2 50. All subscriptions at the above rate must be paid in advance.

WILLIAM COLEMAN,

DEER Lodge, Montana, Confectioner and Fruiterer, and Dealer in Fixed Ammunition, Guns, Pistols, Tobaccos, Segars, Stationery, Toys and General Variety Goods. Branch House in Pioneer City.

DEER LODGE PLANING MILL SASH & DOOR

FACTORY. Planed Lumber of every description. Seasoned, Planed and Matched Flooring, Seasoned Planed Siding, Seasoned Planed Panel Lumber. Mouldings of every size and pattern. Lath and Shingles are always on hand, or made to order. Wood and Iron Turning, Scroll Sawing and Resawing of every description done to order. Office at Murphy & Co.'s Old Stand, Deer Lodge, M. T.
DANCE & MURPHY.

CHAS. BIELENBERG,

SUCCESSOR to Bielenberg & Prowse, Main street, Deer Lodge. Has the finest Market in the Territory, and is prepared to furnish patrons with the choicest Beef, Mutton, Sausage, Pork, Veal, and every variety of Wild Game to be had in Montana. No effort will be spared to give entire satisfaction in Price and Quality.
CHAS. BIELENBERG.

LIVERY STABLE.

SIGN of the Iron Horse. Main street, Deer Lodge City. H. G. Valiton, Proprietor. The most commodious Stables in the country. A fine lot of elegant Carriages and Buggies, fine Teams, and excellent Saddle Horses. A Herd is kept in connection with the Stables.
H. G. VALITON.

THOMPSON & TALBOT'S SALOON,

NEXT door to the Scott House, Deer Lodge, M. T. None but the very best of Liquors and Cigars kept in the House. Billiards and Club Room attached.

CLAGETT & DIXON,

ATTORNEYS and Counsellors-at-Law, Deer Lodge, Montana, practice in all Courts of the Territory.

O. B. WHITFORD, M. D.,

OFFERS his Professional Services to the Citizens of Deer Lodge and vicinity. Office one door south of Bielenberg & Prouse's butcher shop.

CONRAD KOHRS,

BREEDER of and Dealer in fine Cattle and Horses. Thoroughbred Short Horn Durham Cattle bought and sold. Parties wishing to buy or sell will do well to address me.

D. P. NEWCOMER,

ATTORNEY and Counsellor-at-Law, Deer Lodge City, Montana, will Practice in all Courts in the Territory.

L. E. HOLMES, M.D.,

SURGEON and Physician. Office on Main street, next door north of the Post office, Deer Lodge City, Montana.

DEER LODGE BUSINESS DIRECTORY.

BANK EXCHANGE,

PHIL. M'GOVERN, Proprietor. The Bar is supplied with all the best Brands of Wines, Liquors, Cigars, Ale, Porter, &c.

SHARP & NAPTON,

ATTORNEYS and Counsellors-at-Law, Deer Lodge City, Montana, will Practice in all the Courts of the Territory. Office adjoining Wm. Coleman's Store.

J. C. ROBINSON,

ATTORNEY-AT-LAW, Deer Lodge City, Montana, will Practice in all the Courts of the Territory.

JNO. GERBER.   N. DICKENSON.

METROPOLITAN Billiard Hall and Saloon. Gerber & Dickenson, Proprietors. Fine Wines, Liquors, and Cigars, and the best Billiard Tables in Montana.

DEER LODGE BREWERY,

P. VALITON, Proprietor. The Pioneer Brewery, and always ahead! ☞ I am prepared to furnish, Wholesale or Retail, a quality of Beer unsurpassed, if equaled, in Montana. Also Bottled Beer and Bottled Porter, with body, age, and flavor, to commend it to the palate and favor of the most fastidious lovers of Malt Liquors. Orders promptly filled.

BROWN JUG SALOON AND DEER LODGE SODA MANUFACTORY,

V. A. SMITH, Proprietor. Both the Saloon and Soda Works are First Class in every respect, and Customers will find every convenience possible.

R. B. HARRIS,

SIGN of the Red Boot, Main street, Deer Lodge, M. T. Custom-made Boots— the Best in the Territory. Repairing neatly done.

D. S. KENYON,

MAIN STREET, Deer Lodge City, M. T. Groceries, Provisions, Books, Stationery, Notions, and News Depot.

CITY BAKERY AND SALOON,

R. BOISVERT, Proprietor. Fresh Bread, Cakes, and Pies. A good Bar Stock always on hand. Drop in and see me.

JOHN O'NEILL, "404."

DEALER in and manufacturer of Furniture, Matrasses, Bedding. Deer Lodge City, Montana.

C. C. CLAWSON,

DEER LODGE, Montana, will Lecture in the States during the winter. Subjects: THE ENCHANTED LANDS, the Region of the Big Horn and Yellowstone. 2d. The Fire Hole, the Land of Geysers. 3d. The Noble Red Man—Victor the Great, Chief of the Flatheads. The author has an experience of 16 years in the mountains and "knows whereof he speaks." Address, during the winter, Council Bluffs, Iowa, Box 219.

PARCHEN & D'ACHEUL,

SUCCESSORS to Parchen, Paynter & Co., Importers and Jobbers in Pure Drugs, Chemicals, Patent Medicines, Paints, Oils, Varnishes, Stationery, &c. City Drug Store, Main street, Deer Lodge, Montana.

J. L. SWEENEY,

DEALER in and manufacturer of all kinds of Parlor, Kitchen, and Office Furniture. Mattrasses made to order.

BOZEMAN BUSINESS DIRECTORY.

RICH, WILSON & BOGERT,

WHOLESALE and Retail Merchants. Tourists' Supplies, Provisions, Rubber Boots and Clothing. Fine Liquors, Tobacco and Cigars. Wells, Fargo's and Galen's Express. Farmers' and Miners' Supplies. Post-office Corner, Main Street, Bozeman, M. T.

EXCHANGE SALOON,

WILLIAMS & Murray, Proprietors. Best Liquors, Cigars, Wines. A cosy Club Room in connection with the Saloon. Be sure and call on us.

THE AVANT COURIER,

PUBLISHED every Friday, at Bozeman, Gallatin County, M. T. Joseph Wright, Publisher and Proprietor. Terms: One year, in advance or during the first quarter, $6; one year, payable after the first quarter, $8; six months, in advance, $3; six months, during term of subscription, $4; three months, invariably in advance, $2.

METROPOLITAN HOTEL,

BLUM & Engesser, Proprietors. A first-class house. Charges moderate and accommodation superior.

BOTTLER BROTHERS,

AT their Ranch, in the Yellowstone Valley, 34 miles from Bozeman and ?8 miles from the Mammoth Springs, National Park, are prepared to furnish all parties visiting the Park with everything necessary to make the tour pleasant and agreeable, and to act as Guides or Hunters. Their long experience and their thorough knowledge of the country give them great advantages. They are situated an easy day's journey from Bozeman, in a most delightful portion of the valley. Here will be the most convenient place to fit out for the trip, and take Saddle and Pack Horses—which will be always on hand at the most reasonable rates. They are building a hotel, which will be open in the spring, and can entertain Tourists with all the delicacies of the season. Fine Trout and Game of all kinds fill their larder.

A. LAMME & CO.,

MAIN Street, Bozeman, keep all kinds of Supplies and sell at reasonable rates. The fitting out of Tourists made a specialty. Call and see us.

FIRST NATIONAL BANK OF BOZEMAN.

L. M. BLACK, President; Geo. W. Fox, Cashier. Exchange drawn on Helena, Virginia City, Deer Lodge, Corrinne, Salt Lake City, San Francisco, New York, St. Louis, Chicago, Omaha, and on all the principal cities of Europe.

NORTH PACIFIC HOTEL,

GEO. WAKEFIELD, Proprietor, Bozeman, M. T. Tourists and Visitors at Bozeman will find superior accommodation. Daily Coaches from Virginia and Helena. Rates moderate.

HO FOR WONDERLAND!

AND the Mammoth Hot Springs. I am now prepared to carry Invalids and Pleasure Parties to the celebrated Mammoth Hot Springs of Horr & McCartney, and other points in the National Park. G. W. A. Frazier's four-horse conveyance will leave Bozeman weekly, or oftener if necessary, connecting with my trains at the Yellowstone Canyon. For terms, apply to Gov. Williams, Exchange Saloon, Bozeman, M. T.

JOHN WERKS.

MISCELLANEOUS ADVERTISEMENTS.

NICK. CARY,

ADOBE Town, Montana, Wholesale and Retail Dealer in Groceries, Provisions, Liquors, Miners and Farmers' Goods. All goods purchased from first hands for Cash, and sold cheaper than any other house in Madison County. A general outfitting store for everybody. Boots, Shoes, and ready-made Clothing, Gum Boots, etc., etc. Try me.

SEDMAN & McGREGORY,

HOME Park Ranch, Upper Stinkingwater Valley, Madison County, M. T. Breeders of and dealers in Thorough-bred Short-horn Cattle, fine Hogs and Poultry. Thorough-bred and Graded Calves for sale. Chester White and McGee Pigs, Houdan Chickens at prices to suit the times. Our Thoroughbbred stock are selected from the best herds in Kentucky, and our common stock are the best in the Territory. We intend to make Thoroughbred stock-raising a specialty, and guarantee that everything is as represented. Our ranch is one of the best, and we have fitted up our stables, corrals and pastures in the best style. Sedman & McGregory.

MILL CREEK MILLS,

MADISON County, M. T. S. Hall & Co., proprietors. This is exclusively a custom mill, and our customers will be promptly attended to and given satisfaction. It is second to none in the Territory. We claim to make the best flour in Montana. Keep flour and feed on sale at the lowest market price. None but experienced millers employed. We have just commenced the manufacture of Oat Meal and Pearl Barley. Self-rising flour. Give us a trial.

E. & H. T. ANTHONY & CO.,

EMPORIUM of American and Foreign Stereoscopic Views, Photographic Albums, Card Photographs of Celebrities, Foreign and Domestic Chromos, Frames and Passepartouts, Photographic Materials, Stereoscopes, and Lantern Views. A full collection of Yellowstone National Park views. 591 Broadway, New York, opposite the Metropolitan Hotel.

H. H. MOOD,

FARMER and Stock-raiser, Willow Creek, Madison Co., Montana. Horses, Saddles, and a general outfit for National Park Tourists.

MERRIMAN HOUSE,

JEFFERSON City, M. T. First class in all its arrangements. Stages arrive and depart to and from it both Corinne and Helena way daily. Located near the famous silver mines of the Jefferson district. Nathaniel Merriman, Proprietor.

JOAQUIN ABASCAL,

BEARTOWN, Montana, keeps a regular Miners' and Farmers' supply store Buys his goods from first hands, and sells them at a small advance on cost and freight. Everything cheap for Cash—Clothing, Boots and Shoes, Miners' Tools, Groceries, Liquors, etc.

L. W. FRARY,

JESSAMINE Stock Ranch, Madison Co., Montana. Breeder of and Dealer in Thoroughbred and Graded Short-horn Durham Cattle. Choicest breeds of Thorough-bred Fowls. Stock bought and sold.

N. H. WOOD & BRO.,

BEAVERHEAD Valley, Montana, raisers of and dealers in Cattle. Cattle and Horses bought and sold.

SILVER STAR BREWERY,

CHAS. OBERTREIS, Proprietor. Best quality of Beer by the Keg, Gallon, or Glass. Give me a call.

A. CARMICHAEL,

SILVER Star, Montana, dealer in Groceries, Clothing, Hardware, Tinware, Drugs, and a general assortment of Miners and Farmers' Goods.

THE MISSOULIAN.

MISSOULA, Montana. Woody & Turk, Editors and Proprietors. Terms, $6 per year. A first-rate home newspaper. Job work solicited. Send us your subscriptions.

ESTIS HOUSE, WATSON, M. T.

SIM. ESTIS, proprietor. This Hotel is situated at the junction of the Helena, Virginia, Deer Lodge, Bannack, and Corinne Stage Roads, and is kept as a first-class stopping place for coach passengers, tourists, and the traveling public generally. Good fare and clean beds. Coach travel should not miss stopping at the Estis House, as the proprietor spares no pains to set a good table and extend courtesies. Cattle and Horses for sale.

GRAND CENTRAL HOTEL,

OMAHA, Nebraska. Geo. Thrall, proprietor.

BANK EXCHANGE,

BILLIARD Hall, Fred. Peck, proprietor. Bannack City, Montana. Exhilarating beverages carefully compounded. A fine Public Hall in connection with the above. Call on the "Inimitable Fred."

www.ingramcontent.com/pod-product-compliance
Lightning Source LLC
Chambersburg PA
CBHW020313170426
43202CB00008B/587